FACING THE HAKA

The All Blacks perform the haka at the 2011 Rugby World Cup ahead of their clash with France in pool play. PHIL WALTER/AFP VIA GETTY IMAGES

FACING THE HAKA

The challenge, the emotion, the inspiration

ANDY BURT & JAMIE WALL

SYDNEY·MELBOURNE·AUCKLAND·LONDON

Flames erupt as the England team faces the All Blacks haka at Eden Park in June 2014. **DAVID ROGERS/GETTY IMAGES**

To everyone who made this book possible.

At the business end of this project we faced a challenge no one saw coming, but we pulled through and got the job done.

Jamie

To my mum and dad, Kerry and Lynn Burt.

From the frosty early mornings at Fraser Park wearing the green and white hoops of Hutt Valley Marist to the 3am wake-up calls to watch the All Blacks take on South Africa, thank you for introducing me to the wonderful game of rugby and sparking a lifelong passion. Although you are not here to display this book proudly on your coffee table or flick through the pages on a warm Urenui day, I know you will be smiling down and checking for any typos.

Love, Andy

CONTENTS

**FOREWORD/
HE WHAKAPUAKITANGA**
8

PREFACE
11

BEGINNINGS
13

**LEARNING THE
HARD WAY**
25

**TATOU O E TAU
LE TAUA!**
39

THE BULLET
49

**WHEN THE STAKES HAVE
NEVER BEEN HIGHER**
63

**THE GREAT
HAKA REVIVAL**
83

**KIERAN READ
TAKES THE LEAD**
93

THE PRODIGAL SON
107

SEVENS WHĀNAU
117

'KAPA O PANGO'
131

**AN EPIC
ENCOUNTER**
141

**THE HAKA'S HOLLYWOOD
CONNECTION**
149

CHIP ON THE SHOULDER
157

THE PINCER
179

THE LOST HAKA
191

FACING THE BLACK FERNS
203

THE INDLAMU
213

TE TĪMATANGA FOR AN IRISH ICON
225

PASIFIKA POWER
237

FROM LEADING THE HAKA TO FACING IT
247

THE WELSH STALEMATE
257

THE BRAVE BLOSSOMS STARE DOWN THE CHALLENGE
265

THE MEN WHO SUMMONED THE THUNDER
275

ACKNOWLEDGEMENTS
287

FOREWORD

WHETHER PERFORMING HAKA OR on the receiving end of a spirited performance, it is hard to deny that haka moves people; it inspires and unites, and can challenge at times. The reason for this perhaps lies in the essence of what haka is—and that is an outlet whereby an individual or a group can express a deeply held conviction or a strong emotion.

When Te Rauparaha, the famous Māori chief of the Ngāti Toa Rangatira tribe, uttered the now famous words 'Ka mate, ka mate, ka ora, ka ora'—'I am close to death, death is upon me, yet I live still, indeed I am alive!'—he did so in the form of a haka. As 'hā' translates to 'breath' and 'kā' translates to 'ignite', his haka delivery would have been spirited and expressive to all present. He would have been drawing on the deep emotion that a near-death experience brings, having been pursued by a war party intent on his demise. It is haka that gave life to his feelings and emotions.

The Māori world has long used haka to convey important messages, feelings and thoughts across all manner of topics. Tribal matters, political decisions, individuals' actions—noble or otherwise, to name a few. Regardless of the topic, it cannot be denied that haka offers a unique and very Māori way of expressing a group's or individual's position or feeling.

You don't have to look far in Aotearoa to see how deeply fused haka is into the fabric of our country and way of life. Outside of its use in sport, you will regularly see haka performed in the workplace, at schools, weddings, funerals, birthdays and more.

But it is probably the ability of haka to unite, inspire, convey identity and establish connections that has seen haka move beyond the Māori culture to embed itself into the wider Kiwi culture and indeed into the world of rugby.

The association between rugby and haka has a rich history spanning more than 130 years. Since the New Zealand Natives team first performed haka during their tour of Britain in 1888–89, haka has endured and grown across all of rugby. From the All Blacks and Black Ferns to junior clubs and community rugby, haka can be found at all levels of the game.

Some of the most spectacular haka are performed when school First XV rugby teams play their traditional rivals and close to a thousand students are on-field at opposite ends supporting their teams. The New Plymouth Boys' High First XV whole-of-school pre-game haka is truly a sight to behold, with every student in the school lined up on the terraces at Pukekura Park. It is fair to say that haka is so ingrained in rugby that it is hard, if not impossible, to imagine Aotearoa New Zealand rugby without haka.

Now that we know what the haka is and why we do it, we can truly appreciate what it means to face the haka. I look forward to reading this book and finding out what the thoughts, feelings and emotions were of players who have faced up to a haka from one of our mighty teams in black.

—LUKE CRAWFORD, NGĀTI POROU, NGĀTI TŪWHARETOA, MĀORI ALL BLACKS KAUMĀTUA

HE WHAKAPUAKITANGA

AHAKOA HE HAKA TE mahi, he mātakitaki rānei i tētahi haka whakawanawana, e kore e taea te tohe i te mana o te haka ki te whakapukepuke i ngā kare ā-roto, ki te whakaaweawe me te whakakotahi, me te wero anō hoki i ōna wā. Ko te take pea kei roto tonu i te iho o te haka, he huarahi e taea ai e te tangata, e te kapa rānei, te whakapuaki i ngā whakapono me ngā karekarenga ngākau.

I te wā i a Te Rauparaha, te rangatira Māori rongonui o te iwi o Ngāti Toa Rangatira, ka kī ake i ngā kupu 'Ka mate, ka mate, ka ora, ka ora' i whakapuakina mā roto mai i te haka.

Ko te 'hā' he kupu mō te 'hauhā' ō te tangata, ā, ko te 'kā' he kupu mō te 'hikanga o te ahi', ā, kāore e kore ko tana haka he mea wana, he mea whakangahau i ngā kaimātakitaki. Ka tākirikirihia e ia ngā tauwharewharenga o te ngākau mā roto mai i ngā kōrero mō ōna wheako i te tatanga o tana rirongo ki a Aituā i a ia e arungia ana e tētahi ope taua kia patua ia kia mate. Nā te haka ōna kare ā-roto i whakaora mai.

Kua roa te ao Māori e whakamahi ana i te haka ki te whakapuaki kōrero, kare ā-roto, whakaaro hoki mō ngā kaupapa huhua. Ko ngā take ā-iwi, ngā whakatau tōrangapū, ngā mahi ā te tangata—ahakoa pai, kāore rānei—ētahi o ngā kaupapa. Ahakoa te kaupapa, kāore pea e taea te tohe i te āheinga o te haka ki te tuku i tētahi huarahi whakapuaki kōrero mā te rōpū, mā te tangata rānei.

Ehara i te mea me ruku hōhonu te tangata ki te ahurea o Aotearoa ki te kite i te whenumitanga o te haka ki roto i te kahu o te whenua nei me ngā āhuatanga ō ia rā. Hāunga rā ia ōna whakamahinga i te rāngai hākinakina, ka kitea hoki te haka i ngā wāhi mahi, i ngā kura, ngā mārena, ngā tangihanga, ngā huritau, me te nui noa atu o ngā kaupapa.

Heoi anō, ko te āheinga pea o te haka ki te whakakotahi, ki te whakaaweawe, ki te whakapuaki ahurea me te whakahonohono tāngata te take kua whakawhiti te haka i ngā tawhā o te ahurea Māori kia tangata whenua ai tōna noho ki roto i te ahurea Kiwi, ā horapa ana ki te ao whutupaoro.

He hononga mauroa tō te whutupaoro me te haka nō roto mai i ngā tau 130 ka hori. Mai i te wā i haka te Kapa Taketake o Aotearoa i a rātou e karore ana i Piritana i ngā tau 1888–89, kua tānekaha te haka, kua whanake puta noa i te ao whutupaoro. Mai i te Kapa ŌPango ki te Kapa Mamaku, ki ngā karapu ihupuku, me ngā kapa hapori, ka kitea te haka i ngā taumata katoa o te kēmu.

Ko ētahi o ngā haka wana ake nei he mea haka nā ngā kapa whutupaoro ā-kura i a rātou ka tuki ki ō rātou hoariri mauroa, tata ki te kotahi mano ngā tauira i te papa tākaro e tū ātete ana ki te tautoko i ō rātou kapa. Katahi te mea whakamīharo ki te kite i ngā tauira katoa o te Kura Tamatāne o Ngāmotu e whata mai ana i ngā parehua o te papa rēhia o Pukekura ki te haka i mua i te tukinga.

Ka taea pea te kī, nā te nui o ngā here o te haka ki te whutupaoro, me uaua ka wetekina kia mahue te haka i te ao whutupaoro o Aotearoa.

Nā, kua mōhio tātou he aha te haka me ngā take e hakaina ai te haka, kua mārama pea te wheako o te tū ki mua i te mura o te haka.

E hīkaka ana ahau ki te pānui i tēnei pukapuka me te kite he aha ngā whakaaro me ngā kare ā-roto o ngā kaitākaro kua tū ki te ngutu ahi o te haka ā ō tātou kapa mau pango.

—LUKE CRAWFORD, NGĀTI POROU, NGĀTI TŪWHARETOA, KAUMĀTUA O TE KAPA ŌPANGO MĀORI

The All Blacks and England face off before their match at Twickenham in November 2018. HENRY BROWNE/GETTY IMAGES

PREFACE

IN JULY OF 2019, Andy Burt and I were waiting impatiently in the Westpac Stadium press conference room for the post-match interviews after a drawn test match between the All Blacks and the Springboks. He leaned over and asked me what I thought of an idea he had: a book about great All Blacks matches from the perspective of the opposition, with a particular focus on what it was like to stare down one of the most famous rituals in world sport.

I was hooked. This was something special, having its genesis in the bowels of the All Blacks environment. We could bring these stories to the page using some of the most iconic images ever taken, both of the haka and of the games themselves. I'd spent the previous two years travelling with the team as a journalist (plus my entire life watching them as a rugby fan), so I knew full well the electric atmosphere that engulfs every stadium they visit when the team forms up for the haka.

In Buenos Aires and Tokyo, it is met with reverential silence. In Sydney, a rolling thunder of cheers from the thousands of Kiwis in the crowd as it reaches its climax. In London, Dublin and South Africa, a wall of noise as the home fans do their best to counter the challenge with one of their own. It's something that causes debate, especially in the UK, often over how it apparently gives the All Blacks an unfair advantage—which is ironic given its rugby-related origins.

We have treated the subject with the care and respect it deserves, while shedding new light on old stories and new. In the case of 'Kapa O Pango', the All Blacks haka that debuted in 2005, it is protected so fiercely by the team that the use of images of that haka being performed is severely restricted—something we have had to work around.

This is a book that could easily have been 10 times as long as it is. Every haka in the modern era is a special event—not only for the All Blacks but also for their opposition, with many claiming that it is indeed the highlight of their careers. The book evolved from simply telling the tales of those who face the haka to include the perspective of the players who perform it as well, and expanded to include New Zealand's other representative rugby teams.

Here is what the haka, and the fearsome battles that followed it, meant to those out in the middle of the park.

—JAMIE WALL, AUGUST 2020

BEGINNINGS

Opposite The 1919 New Zealand Services team performs the haka, led by West Indian-born Ranji Wilson. **NZ RUGBY MUSEUM**

'Their war-cry was terrible, but it was not so full of terrors as their play.'
—*AUCKLAND STAR*, 13 DECEMBER 1905

LIKE ALL RUGBY STORIES, that of the haka has a few narratives that are held up as gospel, with little attention paid to the nuances in the rest of the story. Many rugby followers, both in New Zealand and overseas, recall it as a pre-game ritual that was performed for the crowd when the All Blacks toured back in the old days. Then, it was a curiosity for onlookers and an obligation for the players, and there's no better evidence of that than the now infamous footage from one memorable game in 1973.

The All Blacks of that year had some mixed results on their tour of the UK in the northern winter of 1972–73. It should be noted that the early 1970s was a difficult period for the side, with series losses to the Springboks and the British Lions coming in successive years—meaning that New Zealanders could not claim to be the best in the world at their own national sport. On the tour, while they'd managed wins over England, Scotland and Wales, they'd drawn with Ireland, lost three and drawn one of their midweek games. Not a bad return, given that the tour was an arduous 30 matches and almost four months long. But not great, either—and this tour would be remembered most for the sending home of prop Keith Murdoch after the win against Wales, a journey that he never completed. Murdoch, who had scored a crucial try in the test, was found guilty of assaulting a security guard in a Cardiff hotel in the early hours of the morning following the game. His subsequent shaming and ordering back across the world saw Murdoch do a bunk in Singapore and then travel on to make a new life in Australia's Northern Territory.

Almost two months after the Murdoch incident, the All Blacks found themselves back on Cardiff Arms Park to play the Barbarians, with the composite side featuring an awful lot of players who had been on the successful British Lions tour to New Zealand in 1971. While the game is mainly remembered for opening with what is rightfully regarded as perhaps the greatest try of all time, the second-most replayed part of the Baabaas' first-ever win over the All Blacks is a very ropey-looking haka performed for the crowd before the kick-off.

If you subscribe to any rugby highlights Facebook page, there is no doubt that it will have popped up in your timeline, usually in response to a fearsome All Blacks haka performed in the present day. It shows the team, full of legendary All Blacks like Grizz Wyllie, Bryan Williams, Ian Kirkpatrick and Bruce Robertson, facing the Cardiff Arms Park stand about 15 metres in from the touchline while the Baabaas continue their warm-up behind them. The team is standing in a

Opposite An impression of the sights and sounds of a tour game. NZ RUGBY MUSEUM

line, looking nervously towards Sid Going as he leads 'Ka Mate'. Clearly, no preparation has been put in by the All Blacks; this is notably evident in the performance of future coach Wyllie, who manages to do almost every action wrong save for the jump at the end. The only consolation for Wyllie is that he's by no means alone in being lost. Only Tane Norton actually looks like he knows what he's doing, while all around him the wrong arms are slapped and the wrong legs stomped.

It's not a great look. While it got a tremendous cheer from the Welsh crowd at its conclusion, the 1973 Cardiff Arms Park haka has gone down in history for all the wrong reasons. It's not something that will grace any All Blacks TV promos any time soon, given that they only show the haka from recent times. That's because the general consensus is that the haka as a challenge to the opposition came into being at the behest of one of the players in the late 1980s, and from that time on it has evolved to become an integral part of the team's image worldwide. As usual, there's more to it than that: one of the first instances of the haka being linked to a New Zealand rugby team took place so long ago that it pre-dates the All Blacks themselves.

Eighty-five years before Wyllie and co. did their haka on Cardiff Arms Park, there was another team in black that travelled the British Isles and did a cultural performance for the benefit of curious onlookers. The team was the New Zealand Natives side, who had undertaken a 13-month, 107-game tour of the UK, Australia and New Zealand itself. The year was 1888, when the British Empire was at its absolute zenith. Queen Victoria was by now the Empress of India as well, putting her in charge of an area of the Earth on which the sun famously never set. Cecil Rhodes, one of the most instrumental proponents of imperialism, declared that to be born British was 'to have drawn the greatest prize in the lottery of life'.

It was this sort of environment that bred the thinking that, while the lands that had been conquered and colonised had unique cultures, they were lower in the natural order of things because Britain ruled supreme. Once these countries had been put down by force in the series of rather one-sided colonial wars of conquest, they were more of a curiosity than anything else. New Zealand was one such, having been opened up for colonisation by the British in the early nineteenth century. While the Treaty of Waitangi was signed in 1840 and seemingly made provision for the land rights of the Māori people to be

> There is at least a solid reason for the 1973 Cardiff Arms Park haka being so woeful. As the team set out from New Zealand, All Blacks manager Ernie Todd had decreed that the haka was not going to be performed at all on the tour. However, the festival nature of the Barbarians fixture meant that the Welsh Union made a special plea for the famous challenge to be performed. Unfortunately, they waited until the night before the game to ask, which meant that the All Blacks (most of whom had never done it before) had no time to practise.

> Despite being 107 games long, the Natives tour party only consisted of 26 players. As well as the four Warbrick brothers, George, Henry and William Wynyard also made up a large chunk of the squad. One game was so affected by rain that the team wore raincoats in the second half, while another match was preceded by a champagne lunch put on by a local nobleman; several of the Natives players were found asleep under a tree prior to kick-off.

safeguarded, by the 1860s this article was being blithely disregarded by the colonial government and subsequently led to a series of conflicts known as the Land Wars.

Precious goods from around the Empire made their way back to the British Isles, as well as its newly acquired citizens. The first Māori to visit was Moehanga of the Ngāpuhi iwi in 1806, who was presented to King George III. But while there had been more travellers on board various British ships, it is fair to say that the average Londoner would still have treated any foreigner with a great deal of curiosity by the time the Natives team arrived. In Greg Ryan's book *Forerunners of the All Blacks* he describes the environment in London:

> Although there had been some black slaves in London during the eighteenth century, and small communities of foreign seamen, students and traders had appeared by the 1880s, few in Britain had seen non-white people at close quarters or knew anything about the distant lands they came from. Most based their ideas on books that contained inaccurate information and sensational illustrations . . . with this level of knowledge and contact, it was easy for speculators to make money parading various 'natives' before a fascinated public.

There had been a very successful exhibition of colonial culture in 1886, when the Colonial and Indian Exhibition was held in South Kensington. Among other displays from the Empire, there was a re-created tomb of Ngāti Pikiao chief Te Waata Taranui, as well as a pātaka (storehouse) from Te Arawa, extensive collections of woven mats, models of waka, and cases of adzes and weapons. So there was at least some knowledge of what sort of society lay half a world away in the South Pacific—among those who could afford to take in such a spectacle.

Yet, given the lack of education among the general population of the time, it was hardly surprising that a great many spectators who came to watch the Natives side play would have been anticipating a horde of savages taking the field. They were to be disappointed—the Natives side dressed and behaved more or less the same as everyone else in Britain at the time, given that New Zealand had been colonised for the better part of a century. It was originally conceived as a purely Māori team, but a lack of available players meant that several Pākehā were drafted in as well. However, this didn't prevent the tour organisers from attempting to cash in on the British expectations.

That's because the Natives tour was being run as a money-making exercise. This was before the formation of a governing body for the sport in New Zealand, so the side was privately run rather than picked by official selection. In fact Joe Warbrick, the captain, simply enlisted the help of his three brothers to fill a few jerseys. The idea was that by negotiating a percentage of the gate takings of each fixture, the organisers could return home wealthy men, which is why the tour itself ran to such an absurd length. This meant that it would need a bit more than just the promise of a good game to help get people through those gates. If the locals were intrigued by the ways and customs of the colonies, then that's what the rugby team would give them a taste of.

Consequently, it was 'announced before the tour that the team would perform a haka prior to each match and that they were taking elaborate mats and other traditional costume to embellish the performance'. This wasn't an original idea. In 1867, a cricket team known as the Australian Aboriginals toured Great Britain and would regularly stage exhibitions of boomerang- and spear-throwing before and after their matches.

But the haka that the Natives team performed, called 'Ake Ake Kia Kaha', was something very new to those in attendance, and upon seeing it for the first time the reaction from the local press was more bemusement than anything else. 'The Maori football team in England appear to combine the best elements of a football team and a circus. When they go on the ground they have their mats and rugs on and they dance a war-dance and sing a war-song before beginning play,' reported the *Bulletin*.

Nevertheless, the haka remained an integral part of the team's protocol for the duration of the arduous tour. The Natives returned to New Zealand in August of 1889, bringing with them a new era for the game at home. Their groundbreaking move to go it alone and tour forced the provincial unions to form the New Zealand Rugby Football Union, which adopted the Natives' black jerseys with a silver fern emblem as the official uniform of the national team. They wouldn't be known as the 'All Blacks' until 1905, though—when the side returned to Great Britain for one of the most storied and famous tours ever.

THE 1905 'ORIGINALS' HAVE become an almost mythical foundation on which the entire All Blacks ethos is based. They played up-tempo, physical and innovative rugby that simply blew opponents off the park. Crowds flocked to watch them play. Their captain, Dave Gallaher, has gone down in New Zealand history not just as a great leader of men, but also as a fallen war hero. Most tellingly, they were denied their shot at perfection in the last test of the tour, meaning that, ever since, the All Blacks have been striving to achieve the impossible goal of putting on the perfect performance.

While the 35-match schedule was still a big ask by today's standards (especially given the medical conditions of the time), it was at least a severe reduction from the frankly ridiculous 107-match itinerary of the team that had gone before them. The gap between 1888 and 1905 in terms of technology means that we have actual movie footage and a plethora of images of the Originals tour, showing a side with a steely determination in their eyes whenever they took the field. After smashing their way through their first 14 matches, they had scored 461 points and conceded only 15. Their opponent on 4 November 1905 was Blackheath in front of a crowd of 15,000 at the Rectory Field in London. According to the *Auckland Star*, 'the colonials [had] fairly taken the metropolis by storm'. But the Blackheath game was also the one where the All Blacks laid down a challenge before kick-off, in front of a stand specially designated for New Zealand supporters.

> For the first time, too, the team treated an English crowd to their Maori haka by way of salutation to their opponents. Halting in front of the New Zealand stand, they welcomed the Blackheath men with the old chant which representative teams in New Zealand have

long since made their own, beginning 'Ka mate, ka mate! Ka ora, ka ora' and ending in a fearsome yell. Their war-cry was terrible, but it was not so full of terrors as their play.

The score at full-time was a resounding 32–0 win for the All Blacks. The *Daily Telegraph* reported:

> The backs, or more particularly the five eighths, often ran with a directness that our players, who had a strange tendency to make for touch rather than the goal line, might take to heart; and when the moment made for a concerted movement, the men raced away at great pace, passing with a precision that was paralysing. It has long been clear that club and county sides have little chance against the New Zealanders, and on form shown in last season's international encounters it may be doubted that representative fifteens will be able to hold their own.

Of course, that prediction was to prove to be pretty spot on, at least for the first three tests. The All Blacks first beat a strong Scotland side 12–7 in Inverleith, before crossing the Irish Sea to Dublin. There they beat Ireland 15–0, before heading back to Crystal Palace in London to defeat England by the same score. The haka was performed before the Scottish test, but not again until what is widely regarded as the tour's climax: the test against Wales in Cardiff.

By now the All Blacks were 25 games into their schedule, with most breaks between fixtures being only around three days. The Welsh were easily the best international side in the UK at the time,

Opposite Bob Deans and George Gillett practise their passing. NZ RUGBY MUSEUM

and would go on to be undefeated in the Home Nations Championship, which these days we call the Six Nations. A crowd of forty or fifty thousand attended the match. This was to be the sporting showdown of the year, and one that would live long in the memories of all there to witness it. The locals expected the All Blacks to perform the haka, so the visitors obliged; but in response the Welsh laid down a challenge of their own.

Thomas Williams had played in Wales' first-ever international win, over Ireland in 1882. By 1905 he had retired from playing and become an administrator with the Welsh Football Union (as the Welsh Rugby Union was originally known), rising to the role of team selector by the time of the Originals tour. Williams then came up with a revolutionary idea that wouldn't change just the game of rugby, but indeed all of international sport. He felt that the crowd had to do something special and unique of their own to counter the New Zealanders' challenge by singing 'Hen Wlad Fy Nhadau'—'Land of My Fathers'. The local newspaper, the *Western Leader*, published Williams' thoughts under the heading 'An Interesting Suggestion' in their edition on the morning of the match, 16 December 1905. (Headlines like that must have been catchy back in those days, because history suggests that plenty of people read it.)

Crowds singing at sports fixtures, whether rugby or otherwise, wasn't anything new. But players and crowd joining in unison to sing a patriotic ode to their country before a game had never been considered before. Thus, after the All Blacks had completed their version of 'Ka Mate', the impromptu rendition of the now iconic Welsh song became the first instance of a national anthem being sung before a game. Not only did it carry that distinction, but it was also the template for how to respond to the haka from then on.

Gwlad!, GWLAD!, pleidiol wyf i'm gwlad.
Tra môr yn fur i'r bur hoff bau,
O bydded i'r hen iaith barhau.

The verses rang out across the field of Cardiff Arms Park. This was going to be a different sort of match for the All Blacks, not least because the Welsh were clearly a better side than every other team they'd trounced so far on the tour. They would be held scoreless for the entire match, with the Welsh scoring a try through Teddy Morgan to take the game 3–0.

In the twenty-fifth minute, Welsh scrum half Dicky Owen released the ball to Cliff Pritchard, who received it at ankle level before darting forward. Having passed by Bob Deans, Pritchard released to Rhys Gabe who in turn found Morgan. Morgan dummied George Gillett and touched the ball down in the corner.

In response, the All Blacks came agonisingly close to scoring an equaliser and possible winner through Bob Deans late in the game; it was famously disallowed as the referee, John Dallas, deemed it to be grounded short—never mind that he wasn't wearing boots and couldn't keep up with the play. This decision set off a long, long controversy that persists to this day, mainly because the result spoiled what would have been an inaugural 'Grand Slam' for the All Blacks.

That's what the first-ever test match between

Opposite top The 'Originals' lineup that took on Wales in 1905. NZ RUGBY MUSEUM

Opposite below The Originals pack down a scrum against Middlesex at Stamford Bridge. NZ RUGBY MUSEUM

Wales and the All Blacks is remembered for, and it would take another 19 years for the next one to happen. But the notion of singing a national anthem stuck, and it also meant that 'Hen Wlad Fy Nhadau' officially became the national anthem of Wales. So, technically, every time a team sings their national anthem when they play the All Blacks, it's a response to the challenge of the haka itself—because rugby is all about tradition.

The anthem didn't go down well with everyone back in 1905, though. A letter to the editor in the *London Opinion* following the game carried an ironic message from one English correspondent, a Mr S.J. Pryor, who felt that the singing by the Welsh crowd was too much:

> Was it a fair deal to the New Zealanders? Was it playing a game to get them on the ground ostensibly to meet a team of Welsh football players, and then set fifty thousand fierce Welshmen to vociferate Welsh songs at them? I hesitate to mention it, and I do not actually suggest it, but it seems very much like intimidation of the worst sort.

The letter writer then went on to have a whinge about having to put up with Welsh buskers singing to him whenever he visited the Principality, so it's likely that Pryor was simply taking the opportunity to have a pop at his neighbours for reasons best known to himself. He probably would have cheered up a bit when his English side started singing 'God Save the Queen' before their games from then on, but the enduring legacy of the Welsh crowd is what gave their side its crucial identity. No Wales rugby experience would be complete without the singing, just as the All Blacks would never be the same without the haka.

The song's last phrase, 'o bydded i'r hen iaith barhau', translates to 'may our old language endure'. This is the window into Welsh culture that the world gets to see—it's more than just a rugby tradition—and it all started as a response to the cultural performance of a group of New Zealanders. While it would take a few more years yet for the All Blacks haka to become what it is today, that signal moment in 1905 meant that Cardiff Arms Park would swell with the united voices of Welsh fans from then onwards.

It is a nice myth that the All Blacks got their name from a journalistic typo during the tour, when a newspaper tried to say they played like 'all backs' due to their enterprise, but which went to print as 'all blacks'. Unfortunately, it isn't based in any fact. The truth of the origin of the name is, like so many others, the most obvious. Teams back in those days were simply referred to by the colours they wore, as seen with American pro teams like the Boston Red Sox or Cincinnati Reds. The All Blacks wore, obviously, all black. The first use of the name by newspapers came about a month into the 1905 tour, and by the end the moniker had stuck.

LEARNING THE HARD WAY

Opposite John Eales breaks All Blacks' hearts in 2000 with his last-play penalty goal. **SCOTT BARBOUR/ ALLSPORT**

6 July 1996
Athletic Park, Wellington

All Blacks 43
(Michael Jones, Christian Cullen, Justin Marshall, Zinzan Brooke, Jeff Wilson, Jonah Lomu tries; Andrew Mehrtens 3 pen, 2 con)

Wallabies 6
(Matt Burke 2 pen)

All Blacks

- 15 Christian Cullen
- 14 Jeff Wilson
- 13 Frank Bunce
- 12 Walter Little
- 11 Jonah Lomu
- 10 Andrew Mehrtens
- 9 Justin Marshall
- 8 Zinzan Brooke
- 7 Josh Kronfeld
- 6 Michael Jones
- 5 Robin Brooke
- 4 Ian Jones
- 3 Olo Brown
- 2 Sean Fitzpatrick (c)
- 1 Craig Dowd

Reserves

- 16 Eric Rush
- 17 Norm Hewitt
- 18 Scott McLeod
- 19 Jon Preston
- 20 Blair Larsen
- 21 Mark Allen

Wallabies

- 15 Matt Burke
- 14 Ben Tune
- 13 Joe Roff
- 12 Tim Horan
- 11 David Campese
- 10 Scott Bowen
- 9 Sam Payne
- 8 Michael Brial
- 7 David Wilson
- 6 Owen Finegan
- 5 John Eales (c)
- 4 Garrick Morgan
- 3 Dan Crowley
- 2 Michael Foley
- 1 Richard Harry

Reserves

- 16 Stephen Larkham
- 17 Pat Howard
- 18 George Gregan
- 19 Daniel Manu
- 20 Andrew Heath
- 21 Marco Caputo

John Eales leads his team out onto the field for their ill-fated 1996 Tri Nations match at Athletic Park.
GETTY IMAGES

'You look back at certain things in your life and think, *Oh, I wish I didn't do that.*'
—JOHN EALES, WALLABIES CAPTAIN

JOHN EALES HAS MORE than enough to feel proud about in his decade-long test career as a Wallaby. For a start he can claim that he's won the Bledisloe Cup, which no Australian test player from 2003 onwards can. Then there's the World Cup, which he lifted aloft as a 21-year-old in 1991, then as captain in 1999. Oh, and the fact that he was a six-foot-seven lock forward who could also kick goals—including one of the most important in Bledisloe history in 2000, which meant that the cup stayed in Australian hands.

The sight of Eales gracefully moving in on the ball at Wellington's WestpacTrust Stadium as time expired is burned pretty hard into the minds of All Blacks fans of a certain age. It was the end of an epic test, indeed an epic series. The first match, in Sydney, had immediately been dubbed maybe the greatest game of all time. The All Blacks struck first with a flurry of tries to lead 24–0, only to see the Wallabies wipe out the deficit by half-time and lead 35–34 with a couple of minutes left. It took a basketball pass from Taine Randell and a trademark run by Jonah Lomu to steal victory for the All Blacks in front of a Stadium Australia crowd of 109,874.

That was a world record. The week after in Wellington saw another stunning try, this time to Christian Cullen, who got on the end of an intricate backline move that saw the ball change direction five times to score under the posts. There was no full-time hooter in those days—the clock just kept running until the alarm on the ref's wristwatch went off. Unfortunately for the All Blacks, that chime rang just as Jonathan Kaplan's arm shot up for a penalty against them, giving the Wallabies a chance at stealing the game and the Bledisloe Cup back across the Tasman. The score was 23–21. From 30 metres out on an angle to the left of the posts, Eales teed up the ball and struck it, aiming for the right-hand post. The ball curved inwards and tumbled over. Eales raised his arms; the crowd was stunned.

Of course, before each one of those tests, Eales shouldered arms with his tracksuit-clad Wallabies teammates and watched the All Blacks perform 'Ka Mate'. He was only a year out from giving up the game completely and had learned some lessons from all the times he'd faced the Wallabies' most important opponent. One lesson, in particular, from 1996. It was a game that would end up being branded on the psyche of the Australians this time—they'd lost before to the All Blacks, often heavily, but not like this. The test at Athletic Park is venerated by New Zealanders as one of the greatest days in All Blacks history. Not just because of the six tries scored. Not just because

LEARNING THE HARD WAY / 29

Opposite David Campese plays with the ball during the All Blacks haka ahead of the 1991 World Cup semi-final. MARK LEECH/ OFFSIDE/GETTY IMAGES

of the commitment to playing up-tempo, free-flowing rugby in the face of a bitter southerly that drove rain horizontally into the faces of players and spectators alike. Not just because it was one of the most iconic fifteens ever put on a field.

It was because it was the most compelling example ever seen of the All Blacks utterly victimising and tormenting an opponent. Ruthlessness in the extreme, from start to finish, in an environment that would have made the Wallabies wonder why they'd even showed up. It ended 43–6, but the reality is that the result was decided before the game even kicked off.

John Eales was, even in the midst of his illustrious career, a player held in high regard by even the most rabid All Blacks fans. By now he was 25 and captain of the Wallabies, having taken over from Michael Lynagh, who had retired after the failed attempt to defend the World Cup the year before. The Queenslander had developed a reputation as a guy who never really had a bad game and more often than not had an outstanding one. He literally towered over his opposition, winning lineouts, getting stuck in at the tight work, and with an almost unbelievable ability to kick goals as well. Even back then, the Aussies were talking him up as one of their best ever. To New Zealanders, it was pretty clear that this guy could well end up being their version of Colin Meads.

Eales was part of the generation of players whose careers bridged the old and the new: the game he started playing internationally in 1991 ended up being a world away from the one he finished with in 2001—in terms of money, physical requirements, expanded coaching staff. The test at Athletic Park was the first under professionalism for both the All Blacks and the Wallabies. They'd all signed contracts with their respective unions over the summer under the cloud of a rebel organisation headed by media mogul Kerry Packer threatening to do what he did with cricket in the 1970s.

This was no mug Wallabies outfit Eales was in charge of, either. The last time they'd beaten the All Blacks was the famous 1994 test at the Sydney Football Stadium, when George Gregan's collision with Jeff Wilson's midriff jolted the ball away and the Bledisloe Cup back into the Australian trophy cabinet. Although they were rebuilding after Lomu had played a big part in reversing the result in 1995, there was still a good mix of experience and youth. Remember, this was back in the days when a home test for the All Blacks wasn't as much of a foregone conclusion as it is in the twenty-first century. So, while the weather forecast for the test in Wellington was grim all week, there was a chance that the Wallabies could get up for this one. The rain and wind were expected to level things up. Eales won the toss under the grimy and decaying Athletic Park grandstand and chose to take the howling gale at their backs in the first half. But this game was over before it even began.

While the choice to take the wind was a debatable one, with local wisdom dictating that you'd play into it when fresh defensively in the first half then spend the second kicking, the next choice Eales made was something he'd live

While Eales has regretted not facing up to the haka, it's unlikely that David Campese shares his sentiments. The record-breaking Wallabies winger never did acknowledge the challenge during his 101-test career, opting to warm up downfield instead, most notably at Lansdowne Road in Dublin for the 1991 World Cup semi-final. It was that day that Campese scored a stunning solo try and created another for Tim Horan, as the Wallabies beat the All Blacks 16-6 and marched on to claim their first title a week later at Twickenham.

to regret. He'd been instructed by coach Greg Smith to carry on warming up after the anthems, knowing full well that it meant disregarding the haka and potentially infuriating the All Blacks.

Cannons went off as the teams took the field, shaking the decrepit Millard Stand and dislodging a shower of rust on to the huddled masses below. The All Blacks lined up into the teeth of the southerly, which was belting in on a direct course straight from Antarctica. The heavy cotton jerseys, which would become drenched in surface water and mud within minutes of kick-off, formed the familiar semi-circle with Zinzan Brooke at the centre. There were no mics on the field to amplify the noise as the big number 8 called his men into the crouch—*Hi!* But something was off. Where were the Australians?

Eales and his men were scattered around their side of the field, warming up. David Campese, then the world record holder for test tries, took it one step further and went down to his own goalposts to swing his legs. But that's Campo. He went on record plenty of times with his thoughts about the haka—only ever referring to the All Blacks as 'New Zealand' or 'the Blacks'. While he'd done it often before, this would be the second to last time it happened. Campese was due to retire at the end of the 1996 season, and if Eales had instructed him to line up with the rest of the Wallabies, the winger probably would have ignored him.

Surrounding Brooke, slapping their liniment-soaked thighs as the rain lashed their faces, was one of the most formidable All Blacks teams ever assembled. The Auckland front row of Craig Dowd, Olo Brown and skipper Sean Fitzpatrick. Zinzan's brother Robin locking the scrum with Ian Jones. Michael Jones at blindside; Josh Kronfeld on the open. Justin Marshall pairing up with Andrew Mehrtens. Walter Little and Frank Bunce punching holes in the middle of the park. A monster on one wing in Jonah Lomu and a freakish all-rounder on the other in Jeff Wilson. And, oh yeah, a guy called Christian Cullen at the back who had already scored seven tries in three tests.

Unless you were right on the touchline (which you still could do at Athletic Park on the Millard Stand side, as there were no advertising hoardings between the seats and the field), it was impossible

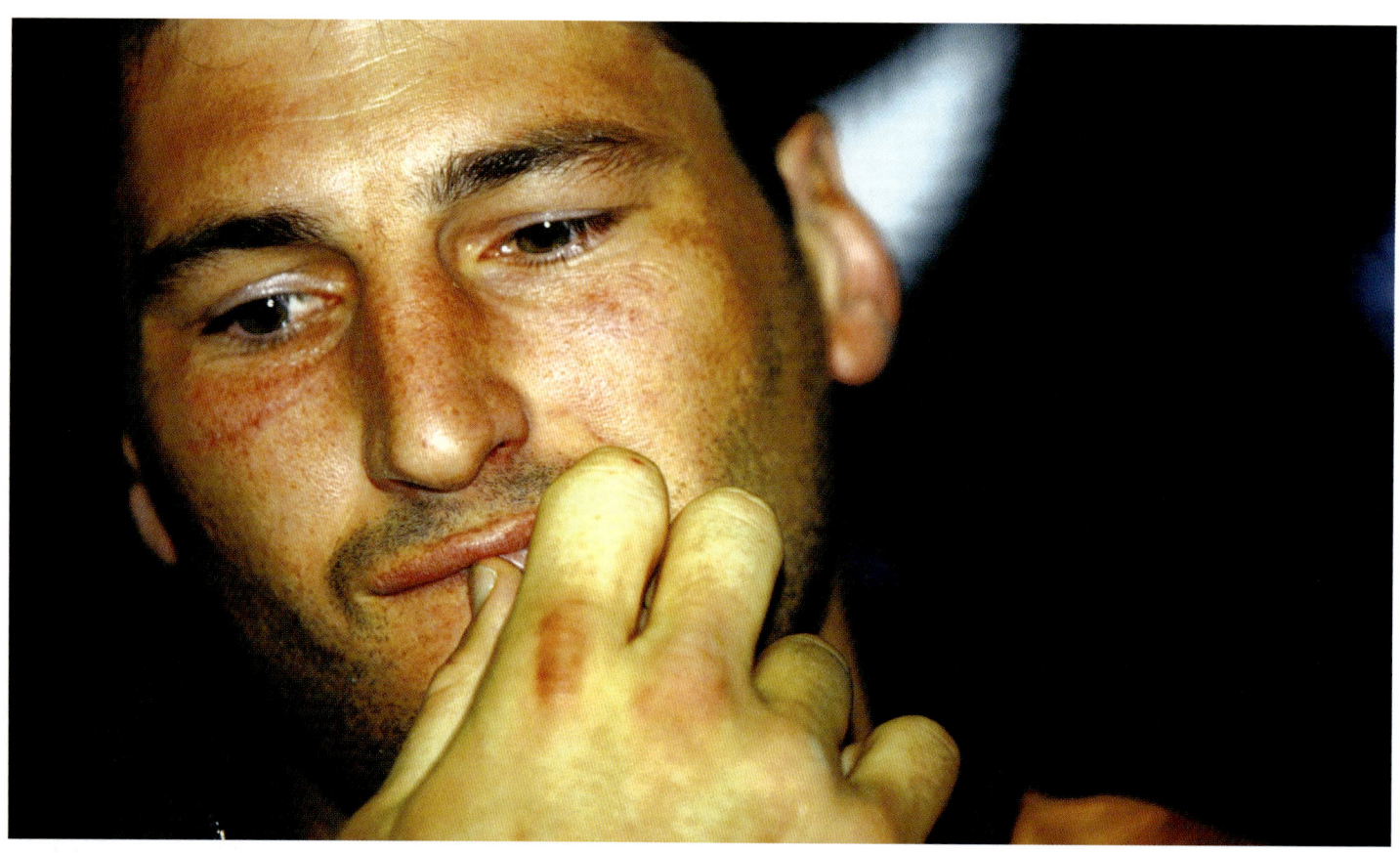

Opposite top John Eales never forgave himself for turning his back on the haka. PHOTOSPORT

Opposite below The Wallabies captain trucks it upfield. NICK WILSON/ALLSPORT

to hear the haka. But the spectators, all 39,000 already soaked to the bone, followed the actions. The shuddering hands, the flexed forearms. The left fists clenched as the right hands cracked into the opposite forearms. The jump in unison—*Hi!*

Then the roar. The cannon was loud, but the crowd's reaction to the haka was louder. All the while, the Wallabies ran grids and attempted to keep warm. The Queenslanders in the team had played on Athletic Park during the first season of Super 12 earlier in the year, but the early start to the season meant that they were greeted then with a typically sunny spring day that was always on the brink of turning sharply cold, as is so well known to any Wellington local.

As far as acts of poor sportsmanship by Australians go, ignoring the haka wouldn't have ranked particularly highly to those in attendance. Most of the fathers who had brought their kids along would be old enough to remember when the 'underarm incident' actually happened, not just Greg Dyer's non-catch in the 1987 Boxing Day cricket test. This was also in the midst of a time period of Australian rugby league clubs making rather suspect medical restrictions on New Zealand players when the Kiwis were due to play the Kangaroos. Besides, what the Aussies did wasn't going to win them the game. In fact, it was about to do the exact opposite.

The All Blacks hit Eales and his Wallabies with a force even harder than the weather event pummelling Wellington over the next 80 minutes. It only took a couple of minutes for Michael Jones to be driven over for the opening try. Then Cullen finished off a sweeping move. Marshall raced half the length of the field into the teeth of the wind. Zinzan picked the ball up off the back of the scrum and waltzed over: 25–6. The All Blacks had the wind, but it was clearly apparent that they didn't need it. The Wallabies needed a miracle, but they were never going to get it in the midst of this ninth circle of hell.

By now, Eales was just another mud-covered Wallaby wondering what exactly was happening all around him. He had to rally his troops behind his own posts six times in total, knowing full well that if they hadn't let the All Blacks get off to such a good start, things might have been a bit different. Deep into the second half, though, all his side could look forward to was a cold dousing under the ancient showers and a beer in the gloomy after-match function room. The final score was 43–6 but the story wasn't over there.

A week later, the two sides met up again at the old Ballymore ground in Brisbane. The conditions were far more what the Australians were accustomed to—no rain or wind and a warm reception from a big home crowd. Again, Smith told Eales to send his troops out for some drills instead of facing the haka, except this time it had a very different effect.

After a tight opening 10 minutes, Ben Tune got his revenge for Jonah Lomu's domination of the week before, bamboozling the biggest name in rugby, turning him inside out and feeding the ball to a recalled George Gregan to dive over and score the first try. It got better for the Wallabies shortly after, with Matt Burke picking up a loose ball on his own 22-metre line, pinning his ears back and haring towards the same corner. For some reason, none of

Eales makes a break during the Bledisloe Cup match in Brisbane, 1996. GETTY IMAGES

> While it's true that the Wallabies haven't developed a challenge to counter the haka in the modern era, that wasn't always the case. Like the All Blacks, the first Australian team to tour the UK performed a 'war dance' for the local crowd, most likely because that's what the locals expected colonials to do. Unfortunately, it was more a concoction of gibberish than anything else. The 1908 Wallabies captain Herbert Moran could scarcely contain his disdain, saying: 'The memory of that war-cry provokes anger in me even after all these years . . . We were officially expected to leap up in the air and make foolish gestures which somebody thought Australian natives might have used in similar circumstances, and we were also given meaningless words which we were to utter savagely during the pantomime. I refused to lead the wretched caricature of a native corroboree, and regularly hid myself among the team, a conscientious objector. None of the men liked it . . . as soon as the business was over some of us rushed to hide our heads in the first available scrum. The final argument used by the Rugby Union [NSWRU—the Australian rugby governing body at the time] was that it had box-office value. The people in England expected it, they said.'

the All Blacks wanted to tackle him—all Burke had to do was gas in one direction for most of the length of the field to score one of the most spectacular tries in test history: 22–9 after half-time. Maybe Smith and Eales were on to something this week. Maybe ignoring the haka just works better when the All Blacks aren't in New Zealand.

Turns out, it only worked for the first hour. This should have been a comfortable win for the Wallabies, a famous turnaround after their humiliation a week before, a stunning show of resilience by a team written off by most and a decent addition to Eales' captaincy achievements. Then the All Blacks decided to shift gears and start playing like the team that would go on to win a series in South Africa for the first time later that season.

Lomu got them rolling in a way that only he could. Sent up the 15-metre line, he carried four tacklers into the Wallabies' 22. Justin Marshall, spotting that he only had Gregan to beat, picked the ball up from the wreckage in Lomu's wake and sniped in to start the All Blacks' comeback. Still a two-score game at 25–16. The All Blacks squared up and rationalised the challenge ahead of them, because it rested on the boot of Andrew Mehrtens. Two chip shots within 10 minutes of one another: 25–22. Then a boomer from 40 metres out as the seconds ticked down. Remember, this was in referee's time in those days. No one knew exactly how much longer there was to play. The Wallabies had actually benefited from a bit of creative timekeeping at the end of their hiding in Wellington—referee Ed Morrison ended the agony a few minutes early, which may well have saved the Aussies conceding 50 points.

Then came the brilliance. A draw was on the cards, but the All Blacks had a scrum 40 metres out with a big open side. Now, if it were these days, with its safety-first approach to such a situation, the only course of action for any team would be to try to grind the opposition scrum and win a penalty. Failing that, take it off the back and use one-out runners until you can catch them offside or they get pinged at a ruck. But this was 1996. Professional rugby had only been around for a matter of months, meaning that coaches and players weren't so worried about minimising risk. Especially not this All Blacks side, when Mehrtens went on a wraparound after Frank Bunce feinted a stock-standard midfield crash. The tiny first five found himself in the same acre of space as Burke in the first half, getting everyone at Ballymore and everyone watching back in New Zealand out of their chairs. On he went. Over the 22. The Wallabies defenders were zeroing in on him—he needed someone to give the ball to.

Mehrtens floated a pass over to Cullen. In a perfect world, the 'Paekākāriki Express' would have held his line and given a pass to Jeff Wilson to score the winner he was denied two years earlier by Gregan in Sydney. But the impetuous fullback put on a right-foot step so big it made him lose his balance. The All Blacks were five metres short. Cullen, who was not exactly renowned in his fledgling career for exploring passing options, looked to have blown it. But he placed the ball so that he could pick it up and keep going, only for Frank Bunce to pinch it away from him and bust through the attention of three more Wallabies to score an unbelievable winner.

Eales and his men once again stood under their own posts as Mehrtens calmly slotted the meaningless conversion. Right then, Eales knew full well that he'd made a mistake before kick-off by not facing the haka—and would carry that burden with him well after retirement.

The game in Wellington in 1996 has gone down in history as one of the great All Blacks performances; the one in Brisbane as one of the great escapes by any team—both featuring an All Blacks team that would, by the end of that year, become known as the 'Incomparables'. But for Eales it would be a lot longer before he addressed the regret he felt about what had happened.

THE PERSON WHO REALLY got on John Eales' case about it was his mum, Rose.

'I didn't want you as captain, our son, to be in that position. It wasn't the done thing. I wondered what the All Blacks thought of it,' she told him. Eales took the maternal criticism to heart and decided to rectify the situation. In 2017, he journeyed to New Zealand to discover what the haka meant and why turning his back on it was such a big deal. On his own initiative, Eales filmed a documentary about the trip, which involved him spending time with former All Blacks captain Wayne 'Buck' Shelford—the man credited with bringing the mana back to the team's haka.

'He's a wonderful guy and he's held with a great deal of respect,' said Eales. 'And you can see why he was such a great leader; he's so firm in his opinions and a very deep thinker about things as well.'

The deeper meaning behind the visit came about when Shelford sent him on a mission to Rotorua to come face to face with a new generation of haka performers. A group of local children performed their challenge to him, as he stood and reflected.

'There is a best way, and the best way is you've got to connect somehow with yourselves. The enduring power of the haka is its ability to connect the team with each other, and also with their heritage, history and their country.'

For a white Australian, it's an interesting proposition to be presented with a display of indigenous culture. It wasn't lost on Eales that the Wallabies didn't have a response for it.

'I think we've started to take some steps towards recognising our indigenous heritage as a nation, more than we have in the past,' he said. 'I think we're some way from finding the right thing to do.'

TATOU O E TAU LE TAUA!

Opposite All Blacks flanker Michael Jones runs at his Sāmoan counterpart Sia Vaifale. **ANDREW CORNAGA/ PHOTOSPORT**

**31 July 1993
Eden Park, Auckland**

All Blacks 35
(Zinzan Brooke, Lee Stensness tries; Grant Fox 7 pen, 2 con)

Western Sāmoa 13
(Anetelea Aiolupo try; Darren Kellett 2 pen, con)

All Blacks		**Western Sāmoa**	
15	John Timu	15	Anetelea Aiolupo
14	John Kirwan	14	Brian Lima
13	Frank Bunce	13	To'o Vaega
12	Lee Stensness	12	Alama Ieremia
11	Va'aiga Tuigamala	11	Lolani Koko
10	Grant Fox	10	Darren Kellett
9	Jon Preston	9	Ofisa Tonu'u
8	Arran Pene	8	Shem Tatupu
7	Michael Jones	7	Apollo Perelini
6	Jamie Joseph	6	Sila Vaifale
5	Robin Brooke	5	Mata'afa Keenan
4	Ian Jones	4	Mark Birtwistle
3	Craig Dowd	3	Peter Fatialofa (c)
2	Sean Fitzpatrick (c)	2	Tala Leiasamaiva'o
1	Graham Purvis	1	Afa Leu'u

Reserves

16	Zinzan Brooke	16	Keneti Sio
17	Walter Little	17	Lio Falaniko
18	Mark Allen	18	Malakai Iupeli
19	Matt Cooper	19	Palamia Lilomaiava

Lolani Koko takes on a bunch of tacklers while Ofisa Tonu'u offers support from his left. ANDREW CORNAGA/PHOTOSPORT

> 'We took the game to the All Blacks and made them work hard.'
> —OFISA TONU'U, WESTERN SĀMOA HALFBACK

IT WAS TWO YEARS after Western Sāmoa had shocked the world. Now, here they were out on Eden Park to finally face the All Blacks in front of a bumper crowd that was evenly supporting both teams. The stage was set for a new era in test rugby—no longer would the All Blacks be playing their home tests against familiar teams like Australia and the British Lions, because now the World Cup had given the previously minnow nations a chance to prove their worth. In 1991 the Western Sāmoa side had done just that, beating Wales on Cardiff Arms Park, narrowly losing to eventual champions the Wallabies and making their way to the quarter-finals.

The following year, things improved again. This was before professional rugby, of course, but it didn't stop New Zealand and Australia organising a precursor to what would eventually be Super Rugby. There had been a tournament called the South Pacific Championship that had run since 1986 but had been disbanded in 1991. It was relaunched as the Super Six in 1992, then the Super 10 in 1993. By that year, the Sāmoans had qualified to compete against undoubtedly the strongest provincial sides in the world, and made a handy go of it. But the greatest match the men in blue would play that season was a test match, finally, against the All Blacks on the biggest rugby ground in New Zealand.

Western Sāmoa had won the Pacific Tri Nations tournament for the third year in a row, beating their old rivals Fiji and Tonga to claim the title. The All Blacks had beaten, somewhat fortuitously, a British Lions side that had nonetheless convincingly taken the second test of the series. However, the Bledisloe Cup had been won back with a very comprehensive win over the Wallabies in Dunedin a fortnight earlier. So the stage was set for the first official test between the nations, even though the Sāmoans had visited twice previously for tours of New Zealand that involved no tests.

A crowd of 38,000 made their way into Eden Park that July afternoon. Auckland is, famously, home to more Sāmoans than Sāmoa itself—so the support for the men in blue meant that they could barely be described as visitors. Besides, all but two of the starting XV lived and played in New Zealand anyway. In fact, captain Peter Fatialofa's Ponsonby club's home ground was within walking distance of Eden Park. Only fullback Anetelea Aiolupo played his rugby in Sāmoa at the time, for the Moata'a club.

The rest of the side featured names that were either very familiar to New Zealand rugby followers at the time or would become so in the coming years. Alongside Ofisa Tonu'u in

Right All Blacks captain Sean Fitzpatrick challenges the Sāmoans in the haka. **ANDREW CORNAGA/ PHOTOSPORT**

Opposite top Lee Stensness scores for the All Blacks. **ANDREW CORNAGA/ PHOTOSPORT**

Opposite below Frank Bunce is lined up by his future All Blacks teammate Alama Ieremia. **ANDREW CORNAGA/PHOTOSPORT**

the backline were Alama Ieremia, To'o Vaega and Brian Lima, who would all go on to have substantial careers in Super Rugby. Hopes were high that both teams would give the ball a bit of air and show off some running rugby.

But first there was the matter of the All Blacks haka squaring off against its first proper test rugby response on New Zealand soil since the Springboks performed the Zulu indlamu before the Second World War. The Siva Tau was composed to be the Western Sāmoa pre-match challenge before their iconic 1991 World Cup run. Translated, it is what you can safely describe as a 'psych-up' chant, with the words 'Tatou o e tau le taua!' literally meaning 'Let's go to war!'

It was now a good few years since Buck Shelford had transformed the All Blacks haka from a crowd-pleasing tradition to a serious warning to the opposition that they were in for a world of hurt over the next 80 minutes. Here was a unique moment in which the opposition were going to fire up with a challenge of their own. But the Sāmoans weren't content to simply do theirs first and sit back to receive the haka—instead both teams launched into their respective challenges simultaneously.

The crowd, now swelling with thousands of Sāmoan, All Blacks and a great deal of other fans who were happy to support both teams, loved it. The sides even managed to choreograph the climactic ending to the haka and Siva Tau together, setting up what would be a historic afternoon.

Opposite Two skippers: Sean Fitzpatrick and Peter Fatialofa. ANDREW CORNAGA/PHOTOSPORT

While the pre-match performance had been spectacular, the same can't really be said of the actual test. This was a tense and closely fought match that contained a great deal of physicality but little in the way of attractive rugby. Fittingly, the one All Black who would be playing his last test match that afternoon dominated proceedings in the way that the rugby world had become accustomed to for most of the past decade. Grant Fox's unerring boot made sure that the All Blacks were ahead from start to finish. Not only that, but it also steered his side down the right end of the park, where the All Blacks could set up camp and score the only try of the first half. Second five Lee Stensness managed to step his way through some serious traffic and dot down, giving the All Blacks a handy 22–6 lead at the break.

However, this wasn't going to be a complete arm wrestle, and the Sāmoans struck back in the second half with one of the best tries seen on Eden Park against the All Blacks. Flanker Sila Vaifale broke out of his 22 and chipped ahead, then regathered inside the All Blacks' 22. Tonu'u fired a wide pass to Mata'afa Keenan, who flicked the ball to Darren Kellett. The first five was hauled down a metre short but popped the ball out for Aiolupo to fittingly dive over in the corner.

Another try to Zinzan Brooke sealed what turned out to be a comfortable scoreline of 35–13. The test was dubbed the 'Battle of the Bandages' for the degree of attrition involved. However, it was a promising enough showing and crowd turnout to get people thinking that they'd see the Sāmoans playing test rugby in New Zealand on a regular basis. That did sort of end up being the case—just not in the way that Sāmoan rugby would have liked.

The truth was that the 1993 test ended up being more of a trial match for future All Blacks than anything else. International eligibility laws were essentially non-existent in those days, and the very next year Wellingtonian Ieremia (along with Sāmoan World Cup first five Stephen Bachop) found themselves pulling on All Blacks jerseys for the home series against the Springboks. Two years later, and Ofisa Tonu'u debuted on the All Blacks tour to South Africa. The two sides would meet again three times over the next seven years, with the team now renamed Manu Sāmoa, each encounter ending in a comfortable All Blacks victory. Then a seven-year gap until 2008, when the All Blacks ran up a century of points in their one-off test match.

Another seven-year gap followed, along with a growing amount of criticism about the All Blacks not having visited Sāmoa itself to play a test. That milestone was finally achieved in 2015, when Manu Sāmoa welcomed the All Blacks to Apia with not only boundless enthusiasm from the local population but also their best performance, ending the contest with the closest scoreline to date between the two sides: 22–16 to the All Blacks.

THE BULLET

Opposite James 'Bullet' Dalton prepares to throw in to a lineout. **DAVID ROGERS/ ALLSPORT**

15 August 1998
Kings Park, Durban

All Blacks 23
(Justin Marshall, Taine Randell tries; Andrew Mehrtens 3 pen, 2 con)

Springboks 24
(James Dalton, Bobby Skinstad, Stefan Terblanche, Joost van der Westhuizen tries; Percy Montgomery 2 con)

All Blacks		**Springboks**	
15	Christian Cullen	15	Percy Montgomery
14	Jeff Wilson	14	Stefan Terblanche
13	Eroni Clarke	13	Andre Snyman
12	Mark Mayerhofler	12	Pieter Muller
11	Jonah Lomu	11	Pieter Rossouw
10	Andrew Mehrtens	10	Henry Honiball
9	Justin Marshall	9	Joost van der Westhuizen
8	Isitolo Maka	8	Gary Teichmann (c)
7	Josh Kronfeld	7	Andre Venter
6	Taine Randell (c)	6	Rassie Erasmus
5	Robin Brooke	5	Mark Andrews
4	Royce Willis	4	Krynauw Otto
3	Olo Brown	3	Adrian Garvey
2	Anton Oliver	2	James Dalton
1	Carl Hoeft	1	Robbie Kempson

Reserves		**Reserves**	
16	Scott Robertson	16	Bobby Skinstad
17	Norm Berryman	17	Ollie le Roux
18	Carlos Spencer	18	Franco Smith
19	Mark Robinson	19	Andrew Aitken
20	Craig Dowd	20	Werner Swanepoel
21	Ian Jones	21	Chester Williams
22	Mark Hammett	22	Naka Drotske

James Dalton scores the match winner in Durban in 1998. DAVID ROGERS/ALLSPORT

'If you weren't switched on facing that haka, you'd never get the chance to switch on during the game. You'd take a beating.'

—JAMES DALTON, SPRINGBOKS HOOKER

IT WAS A YEAR that almost all All Blacks fans want to forget ever happened. Almost all, that is, because one lucky but extremely unpatriotic bastard managed to predict all the teams' results in the Tri Nations tournament and made an absolute killing betting on them. But, for everyone else, 1998 was a season of defeat after defeat, ending up in the second-worst return since 1949. Five times the All Blacks performed the haka to the Wallabies and Springboks; five times it was followed by a crushing failure that ended up with a full public inquisition, a captain trying to hand in his job and a coach nearly losing his.

This All Blacks side was only two seasons removed from dominating the first Tri Nations and the historic series victory over the Springboks. But it was the mere flesh of that side, now missing both its backbone and its brain. The most experienced core of the forwards was gone with the retirement of Sean Fitzpatrick and Zinzan Brooke. Plus Jonah Lomu was out, although no one knew at the time that it was because of a debilitating kidney illness, which would eventually take his life at the tragically young age of 40.

But the turmoil surrounding an All Blacks side that had clearly done little to sustain its dominant run of form in the previous two years didn't take any of the gloss off the victories that were claimed at its expense. In particular that year, there was one man who was to play a pivotal role in the All Blacks' most crushing defeat and enjoyed every last bit of it. James Dalton was 25 years old, weighed around 100 kilograms and stood 1 metre 77 centimetres. His nickname was, indeed still is, 'Bullet'. He was born to play hooker. His 2019 biography, *Bullet Proof: The James Dalton Story* by Mark Keohane, quotes him as saying in 1998:

> It's one of the key roles in any rugby team, not only in terms of technique at scrum and lineout, which are vitally important areas, but in terms of generating some passion and energy right there in the eye of the storm. The hooker is at the centre of everything. You don't need a quiet guy in that position. You need some edge.

Dalton is no stranger to controversy on or off the field. He's faced a number of serious charges over the years.

Dalton had been part of the Springboks team that won the 1995 World Cup, then lost the series to the All Blacks in 1996. He watched on for the majority of those games because he'd been suspended in the World Cup for his part in the infamous 'Battle of Boet Erasmus' against Canada,

Opposite top 'Bullet', a.k.a. James Dalton. DAVID ROGERS/ALLSPORT

Opposite below Corne Krige, Lawrence Sephaka and James Dalton sing the South African national anthem. DAVE ROGERS/ GETTY IMAGES

after he was one of three players sent off for their part in a sideline brawl. It almost had the most dire of consequences when it came to the business end of the tournament, as Dalton's dismissal meant that the Springboks might have had to forfeit their semi-final against France due to the torrential rain in Durban that only let up at the very last possible moment (if the game had been called off, the team with the better disciplinary record would have gone through). But the game went ahead; the Boks won, moved on to the final against the All Blacks and won that one too.

In 1996, Dalton found himself down the pecking order behind veteran John Allan, followed by the extremely questionable selection of Henry Tromp in the defining game of the All Blacks tour. Tromp was convicted of manslaughter in 1993 after a labourer on his family's farm died from injuries sustained during a beating for 'disciplinary reasons'. The notorious Tromp got a start but couldn't go the distance in the epic second test in Pretoria, so replacement hooker Dalton came on for the thrilling last 15 minutes. The All Blacks had shot out to a 24–11 lead at half-time, only to be hit with a Springboks comeback that brought the score back to 27–26. A clutch penalty to Jon Preston and an outrageous dropped goal by Zinzan Brooke pushed the All Blacks' lead to seven points.

'Those final 15 minutes were frantic in that it was all-out South African attack,' Dalton said in *Bullet Proof*. 'The crowd noise was incredible and it was as if 50,000 spectators, plus the 15 Boks on the field, were pushing for a final converted try that could keep the series alive.' Despite an all-out assault on the All Blacks' line to get that last try, the Springboks were denied only a couple of metres short as time ran out on one of the greatest tests ever played. 'They hung on, history was made and my 15 minutes against the All Blacks was not one of fame, but pain.'

Dalton got a start in the last test, after the series had been lost. The Springboks gained some measure of revenge against the All Blacks that day at Ellis Park in Johannesburg, beating them 32–22 in a very flattering scoreline for the visitors. He played in the second of two losses the next year, a crazy game at Eden Park that yielded a scoreline of 55–35 to the All Blacks. Dalton then found himself enjoying a decent run of form for Transvaal later in the season. New Springboks coach Nick Mallett liked what he saw and recalled the hairless hooker to his squad for the South Africans' end-of-year tour, then to take on the All Blacks in Wellington and Durban in 1998's Tri Nations tournament. Playing against the All Blacks was always the highlight of Dalton's international career, as he described in *Bullet Proof*:

> They came with a reputation, with a presence that commands attention. They were like these black knights in armour and the power of the colour was almost invariably matched with the power of their performance. The haka was also thrilling to watch because I saw it as a challenge and an invite to go to battle. Some may view the haka as pre-match entertainment but I saw it as the start to the

Opposite top Pieter Rossouw runs in under the posts to score the try that sealed the match at Athletic Park. ROSS LAND/ GETTY IMAGES

Opposite below Joost van der Westhuizen clears the ball from a ruck. ROSS LAND/GETTY IMAGES

match. If you weren't switched on facing that haka, you'd never get the chance to switch on during the game. You'd take a beating. I was proud to be a Springbok standing there and understanding the significance of the cultural war dance. You weren't just playing an opponent, you were playing legacy, history, culture and then the player.

Dalton was part of a side coming into 1998 on a winning streak. The 90-point Eden Park fixture had actually been the last time they'd lost a test to date, but that fact had flown under the radar of most that packed into Athletic Park on an unusually calm and sunny July day in the capital. The 40,000 who were in attendance were hoping for a repeat of that spectacle, especially as Super 12 was at the height of its high-scoring infancy and Wellington was home to a Hurricanes side that definitely preferred attack rather than defence. The test was also the fiftieth between the two historic rivals. John Hart's All Blacks had started the season with two wins over a legendarily terrible England side in Dunedin and Auckland (it's worth remembering that it was also one that would ultimately provide the nucleus of their eventual World Cup-winning squad in 2003, though), but then dropped the first Bledisloe Cup test against the Wallabies at the Melbourne Cricket Ground.

What the crowd got, however, was a trip back in time to the trench warfare that typified All Blacks versus Springboks rugby down the decades. Dalton and his props Adrian Garvey and Robbie Kempson found themselves colliding with the front row of Craig Dowd, Anton Oliver and Olo Brown more often than not. When the ball did come out of the scrum, they would've barely disengaged with one another before it was booted downfield by either Carlos Spencer or Henry Honiball. The closest anyone had got to scoring a try was Jeff Wilson diving on a kick-through to touch down just before the break, only for referee Ed Morrison to rule that the ball was dead when he did so. At half-time the score looked like something from the 1956 Springboks tour: South Africa 3, New Zealand 0.

As the teams huddled in the middle of the field, it seemed like it might very well stay that way. Hart had taken a gamble on Spencer after Mehrtens' ineffectual display in Melbourne, but it backfired. The Boks shut down his naturally creative game play with ruthless efficiency, then were able to bank on giving away kickable penalties because Spencer had left his kicking boots back at the hotel. Soon after half-time, Hart sent Mehrtens out to try to rectify the situation, which he looked to have done when he immediately levelled the scores with a penalty goal.

Percy Montgomery answered to put the Boks back in the lead, and they then camped out in the All Blacks' half. They hadn't won in New Zealand since 1981, at the same venue. Dalton and his teammates could almost taste the history they were about to make. With 10 minutes to go, they landed the killer blow when they were awarded a scrum just to the left of the posts, 15 metres out from the goal line. Joost van der Westhuizen ran the ball right, Henry Honiball got a pass going

56 / FACING THE HAKA

back the other way, then gave it to Pieter Rossouw who trucked it straight through a yawning gap to dive under the posts. It was all too easy. The Springboks didn't know it yet, but the 13–3 result would be the last time they'd win in New Zealand till 2007.

While that test was the epitome of an unaesthetic grind, befitting of the physical nature of the rivalry between the two sides, the next one would be a very different story. James Dalton would find himself right at the most pivotal moment of the All Blacks' most heartbreaking loss of the young professional era.

Kings Park, Durban—where the goalposts are striped black and white to match the Natal province's colours. Perhaps it gave the All Blacks a bit of a feeling of being at home, as they'd won their last test match there on the 1996 tour and got off to a perfect start a couple of weeks after their defeat in Wellington. Jonah Lomu was back and it seemed like Hart had finally started to get the new-look All Blacks firing on all cylinders. After only six minutes, they pounced on a dusty pass just out from their 22 as the Springboks attacked. The forwards piled over and Justin Marshall quickly got the ball out wide to Lomu.

The big winger never managed to score a try against the Springboks in his entire career, but this was about as close as he got. After storming down the sideline, he was hauled to the ground in a desperate tackle by Rassie Erasmus and Andre Venter, but not before getting a pass away that deflected off the knee of Marshall. The halfback hared after the bouncing ball as it toppled towards

Opposite Jonah Lomu takes on Stefan Terblanche in Durban. DAVID ROGERS/ ALLSPORT

the dead-ball line, just diving on it to score. Taine Randell, who had been made skipper in place of the legendary Sean Fitzpatrick, then scored after a bust up the middle by Isitolo Maka to give the All Blacks a 17–5 lead at half-time.

This is more like it, thought the thousands of sleepy New Zealanders half a world away, watching the game in the early hours of Sunday morning. The fans had sat through four consecutive defeats, because the game after the Wellington loss saw the All Blacks soundly beaten by the Wallabies in Christchurch. Bye-bye Bledisloe Cup. Four times the All Blacks had gone out, performed the haka, then had nothing to show for it 80 minutes later. This was different; this was the righting of the ship. It was about bloody time.

Things got even better in the second half when Mehrtens landed a couple of penalties to make the score 23–5 with only 15 minutes to play. It was going to take something ridiculous to overturn this deficit. What came next has gone down in history as the greatest Springboks fightback of all time.

First, Joost van der Westhuizen scooted from a ruck 10 metres out, touching down under the posts and sprinting back to halfway to resume the battle: 23–12. Then the Boks started rolling. Bang, bang, bang up the middle of the park as van der Westhuizen marshalled his troops. Big South African frames slammed into the All Blacks, carving off metres at a time. Right up to the goal line, where Bobby Skinstad emerged from a pile of bodies over the line to score another try: 23–19 with five minutes to go. Everything was going the home side's way—they'd woken up from their hour-long slumber and could taste another famous win. They still needed a miracle, but it was going to come in the most controversial of circumstances.

The Springboks' chance came when Lomu debatably took out Stefan Terblanche after he'd kicked the ball ahead. This was 1998, when sanctions on foul play were nowhere near the draconian levels of today, so if the hit had occurred at any other point in time in the game it's unlikely that it would've even warranted a replay on the TV coverage. But it was a penalty, and it was shaping up to be the last play of the game. Honiball booted it into the corner and Dalton threw into the lineout straight into the big palms of Krynauw Otto. The forwards stacked up into a textbook drive, splitting their All Blacks opposites and gaining momentum. Bullet found himself loaded into the back, with the ball tucked under his arm. Then, the Boks fired.

Through he went, in a mess of bodies and over the line. Australian referee Peter Marshall had no hesitation, flinging his arm in the air and blasting on his whistle. It was a try. The Springboks had pulled off the impossible, going at over a point a minute for the last stage of the game.

But was it a try? The footage is highly inconclusive, and the immediate reaction of the All Blacks around the scene is one of disbelief. In that sort of pressure situation, it's pretty impossible to manufacture that kind of unified body language. They genuinely believed that the ball had been held up, perhaps not even making it over the line at all. There were some claims afterwards that referee Marshall had mistaken Dalton's bald head for the ball and saw it slide into the turf. It didn't matter,

Opposite Taine Randell takes on Bullet in a tackle. DAVID ROGERS/ALLSPORT

the ref's call stood and the Springboks had beaten the All Blacks for the second time in one season. They hadn't done that since 1976.

'If the TMO [video replay system] had been around then, we would have won the game in Durban,' said John Hart later. He's probably right. But Bullet ended up being the hero of the day, and played a pivotal role in having the 1998 season branded as one of the worst ever in All Blacks history. A week later, the Springboks defeated the Wallabies at Ellis Park to win the Tri Nations for the first-ever time. They would eventually win 17 tests in a row, equalling the then test record for consecutive victories before being beaten by England at Twickenham.

Being part of that era made Dalton one of the most successful Springboks ever, with 35 wins and eight losses in 43 tests by the time he retired in 2002. His teammate Erasmus eventually became coach of the 2019 World Cup-winning Springboks side. That day was immortalised by Siya Kolisi becoming the first black African to hold the trophy aloft, and Dalton, despite his fearsome reputation on the field and wildman one off it, was completely committed to the new direction that South African rugby was taking.

'The transformation has been incredibly successful in the team,' he said. 'Anybody that brings transformation up now [as an issue] is absolutely foolish. We've cut those shackles off once and for all and it's a totally unified rugby team.'

Dalton does retain one quality that exists among the old guard of South African rugby, though: that you're only a real Springbok if you've played the All Blacks. He faced the haka seven times, every one a prelude to what he regarded as the most important tests of his career. Even though the Springboks are now world champions, Dalton still uses the All Blacks as a benchmark, and that is testament to the respect he has for them as a team. He told *Sport24* in 2019:

> Let's take the success and what we've achieved and build on that, and then I do believe that we could possibly win back-to-back World Cups. You look at the All Blacks and they were world No. 1 since 2008 and that's just remarkable.

The Springboks got the better of the All Blacks in 1998, but to do so they had to bring out the best they possibly had.

WHEN THE STAKES HAVE NEVER BEEN HIGHER

Opposite The French refuse to take a backward step as they face the haka in 2007.
JULIEN BEHAL/PA IMAGES VIA GETTY IMAGES

23 October 2011
Eden Park, Auckland

All Blacks 8
(Tony Woodcock try; Stephen Donald pen)

France 7
(Thierry Dusautoir try; François Trinh-Duc con)

All Blacks
- 15 Israel Dagg
- 14 Cory Jane
- 13 Conrad Smith
- 12 Ma'a Nonu
- 11 Richard Kahui
- 10 Aaron Cruden
- 9 Piri Weepu
- 8 Kieran Read
- 7 Richie McCaw (c)
- 6 Jerome Kaino
- 5 Samuel Whitelock
- 4 Brad Thorn
- 3 Owen Franks
- 2 Keven Mealamu
- 1 Tony Woodcock

Reserves
- 16 Andrew Hore
- 17 Ben Franks
- 18 Ali Williams
- 19 Adam Thomson
- 20 Andy Ellis
- 21 Stephen Donald
- 22 Sonny Bill Williams

France
- 15 Maxime Médard
- 14 Vincent Clerc
- 13 Aurélien Rougerie
- 12 Maxime Mermoz
- 11 Alexis Palisson
- 10 Morgan Parra
- 9 Dimitri Yachvili
- 8 Imanol Harinordoquy
- 7 Julien Bonnaire
- 6 Thierry Dusautoir (c)
- 5 Lionel Nallet
- 4 Pascal Papé
- 3 Nicolas Mas
- 2 William Servat
- 1 Jean-Baptiste Poux

Reserves
- 16 Dimitri Szarzewski
- 17 Fabien Barcella
- 18 Julien Pierre
- 19 Fulgence Ouedraogo
- 20 Jean-Marc Doussain
- 21 François Trinh-Duc
- 22 Damien Traille

The French advance on the haka. RYAN PIERSE/GETTY IMAGES

'During the week the players felt they wanted to do something. Many of our players were not there in 2007. We thought about it that morning.'
—THIERRY DUSAUTOIR, FRENCH CAPTAIN

THIS WAS THE GAME that all of New Zealand watched but spent the whole 80 minutes wishing they hadn't. The game that ended with an overwhelming feeling of relief rather than celebration. The game when the nation exhaled as one at the final whistle—the All Blacks were world champions again. Eden Park, 23 October 2011. Finally.

It was the culmination of a dramatic month and a half for the All Blacks. First fives went down like flies. Players were caught on a night out before a crucial knockout game. The expectations of an entire nation rested on a team that hadn't held the World Cup aloft in 24 long years. In their way was a surprising opponent: France, the same foe that strode onto Eden Park in 1987 in the first-ever World Cup final. Not even the most optimistic Frenchman would have predicted that their team would make it all the way to the big dance—after all, they had managed to be thoroughly beaten by the All Blacks in their pool game and then scraped through to the quarter-finals despite losing to Tonga as well. That wasn't the end of their entertainingly Gallic dramas, with a player revolt during pool play that led to coach Marc Lièvremont being effectively sidelined for the remainder of the tournament.

They'd had some good luck thereafter, drawing an English side that was treating the tournament like a stag do. The French muscled out a win against them and then took on Wales in the semi-final. The Welsh, conveniently for the French, had forgotten to bring a goal kicker with them to New Zealand and then had their captain Sam Warburton sent off. Everything was turning up trumps for France, but in the final they had to contend with a home side that hadn't lost on Eden Park in 17 years.

The All Blacks smashed their way through their pool, then found themselves without Dan Carter for the quarter-final against Argentina. His replacement Colin Slade only lasted half an hour of that match, with Piri Weepu having to step in and close the game out with seven penalty goals. Aaron Cruden was then entrusted with the number 10 jersey from there on in, giving an assured display in the semi-final against the Wallabies a week later. So the die had been cast—the All Blacks, after five World Cup disappointments in a row, just had to beat France to claim the trophy.

A crowd of 61,079 squeezed into the largest stadium in New Zealand on the night of the final. While it was holding around 13,000 more than usual thanks to temporary stands behind either set of goalposts, the attendance still wasn't quite as high as the 61,240 that had seen the series

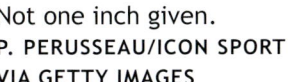

Not one inch given.
P. PERUSSEAU/ICON SPORT VIA GETTY IMAGES

decider between the All Blacks and the Springboks in 1956. There was another comparison to be drawn between those two tests, though. Back in the 1950s, New Zealand and South Africa were regarded as the two contenders for the title of best team in the world, so the fourth test at Eden Park with the series sitting at 2–1 in favour of the All Blacks was essentially a World Cup final 31 years before the first official one.

Then there was the All Blacks' history with France at World Cups. The first time they'd met in a World Cup was that final in 1987, where the peerless All Blacks dismantled the French 29–9 (France shouldn't feel too bad about the score—it was the closest the All Blacks had been pushed in the whole tournament and the first time they'd been held under 30 points). But the second time was quite the opposite. Drawn to face one another in the 1999 World Cup semi-final, the All Blacks and France locked horns for what might be the best game of World Cup rugby ever played—or worst, depending on where you're from. This was only four years since the sport had gone professional, so players hadn't quite turned into the bulky, over-coached robots we often see today. There still seemed to be plenty of space to run the ball, which the All Blacks did to shoot out to a comfortable 24–10 lead in the second half. Game over, you'd have thought, until the French decided to wake up and the All Blacks somehow managed to make all their most costly mistakes in their combined careers over the course of 15 minutes. France cashed in with three tries and eventually won 43–31, with the result costing All Blacks coach John Hart his job and plunging the nation into a deep state of depression.

WHEN THE STAKES HAVE NEVER BEEN HIGHER

Opposite top Freddie Michalak runs away to set up the winning try in 2007. LIEWIG CHRISTIAN/CORBIS VIA GETTY IMAGES

Opposite below France's winger Christophe Dominici, captain Thierry Dusautoir and utility Damien Traille celebrate the 2007 victory. LIEWIG CHRISTIAN/CORBIS VIA GETTY IMAGES

Then, another dose in 2007. This time it was a quarter-final in Cardiff—ironically, part of a tournament mainly hosted by France but the venue of the French side's knockout game thanks to an inept display in the pool rounds that saw them lose to Argentina. This was supposed to be a walk in the park for a strong All Blacks side which, as per usual, had breezed through their pool and were hot favourites to win once again. But fate, or more accurately a fantastic performance from France, got in the way of that.

The French faced the haka that day with something that hadn't been seen before. They'd already won a preliminary psychological battle earlier in the week by opting to play in their dark blue strip, which meant that the All Blacks donned a now infamous grey jersey that is synonymous with failure. When the All Blacks formed up for the challenge, the French removed their tracksuits to reveal red, blue and white t-shirts.

Liberté, égalité, fraternité.

While the haka is sacred to Aotearoa and probably the strongest shop window of culture to the world, the Frenchmen decided to bring out the colours that their modern nation was founded upon. The ones that were paid for by the blood of millions in the Napoleonic and world wars, and the ones that wrap their way through the fearsome lyrics of 'La Marseillaise'. This was a French side that had shown up for battle.

Back in those days, there were no rules about where you were supposed to stand when facing the haka (more on that later). The line of Frenchmen, who now formed a long human *Tricolore*, shouldered arms and advanced to the halfway line. The All Blacks, seeing them approach like La Grande Armée at Austerlitz, moved off their position on the Millennium Stadium 10-metre line and walked up close enough to smell the garlic on the Frenchmen's breath. The crowd, bolstered by thousands of New Zealanders who now called the UK home, roared. This was the sort of fire that was going to ignite this game from a mere walkover to a contest befitting of a World Cup knockout match.

The positioning of the French had another, perhaps unintended but nonetheless powerful, effect. For years, TV camera crews had placed themselves between the two sides, giving a close-up view of the haka from head on—as an opponent would see. Now there was less than a metre of no-man's-land between the two sides, so the perspective had to be from the very end of the line looking down. All Blacks lock Ali Williams walked to the front and threw down his headgear. Having muscled their way into the shot, the haka was no longer about the All Blacks so much as it was about the *Tricolore* and the French response. 'Ka Mate', led by Carl Hayman, rang out as the All Blacks inched their way forward.

The French did as well. Soon there was nothing more than a few inches separating the teams. Because of the All Blacks' low body position as they crouched, the cameramen had no choice. They couldn't shoot the All Blacks from the front,

Opposite top *L'Homme des Cavernes*: Sébastien Chabal. LIEWIG CHRISTIAN/CORBIS VIA GETTY IMAGES

Opposite below Richie McCaw and Graham Henry front the media after the disastrous 2007 Rugby World Cup quarter-final loss. PHIL WALTER/GETTY IMAGES

> The display of French patriotism before the quarter-final wasn't the first time the rugby side had invoked their country's history for motivation. In 1979 the French famously beat the All Blacks for the first time on New Zealand soil at Eden Park, 24-19, and did so on a particularly auspicious date. The test was played on 14 July, Bastille Day. In 1995 the All Blacks toured France and were drawn to play a test on 11 November—Armistice Day. Again, a fired-up French side won, 22-15.

because France were in the way. Instead, they moved around to behind the All Blacks formation and filmed their backs. Instead of the normal front-on view of the haka, what viewers saw was the fearsome look on the French players' faces as they absorbed it and used that to fuel what they were going to do for the next 80 minutes. Right in the middle of the line was the most physically impressive specimen of all, replacement lock Sébastien Chabal. Six foot three, 113 kilograms and owner of the most rugged beard ever seen in test rugby, the French called him 'l'Homme des Cavernes'—'the Caveman'. His teeth snarled through the black beard as he swayed side to side with his fellow players, glowering down at All Blacks halfback Byron Kelleher.

When the All Blacks were finished, the line of Frenchmen broke and turned their backs, but not before Chabal had made sure his opponents knew they were in for a much tougher prospect than anticipated. France's captain, Raphaël Ibañez, even dared to flash a wink before discarding his red shirt and getting in position for kick-off.

But it was the player who was to be the future captain who would leave his mark on this famous fixture. Thierry Dusautoir is a man born of the remnants of French empire. Côte d'Ivoire was a part of the French West African colonies, which is why Dusautoir's heritage can be traced there. He found his way to the French mainland and took up the game at age 16—a veritable lifetime too late for most others with ambitions of playing test rugby. The flanker bounced around the Bordeaux, Colomiers and Biarritz clubs before settling in for a long career at Toulouse that would bring him four French Top 14 championships and two Heineken Cups. By 2007, Dusautoir had established himself as a regular in the French team.

After staring down the haka, he went on to make a record 38 tackles in the game. Dusautoir was everywhere on the Millennium Stadium pitch that day, crunching into All Blacks ball-runners and leaving bruises every time he did so. He played like a man possessed. For good measure, he popped up in the midfield in the fifty-fourth minute to score a crucial try that levelled the scores.

Contrary to what a lot of people might think about this test, it's fair to say that for most of it the All Blacks actually played pretty well. They scored two very good tries through Luke McAlister and Rodney So'oialo and, for the most part, looked like they were going to win what had turned out to be

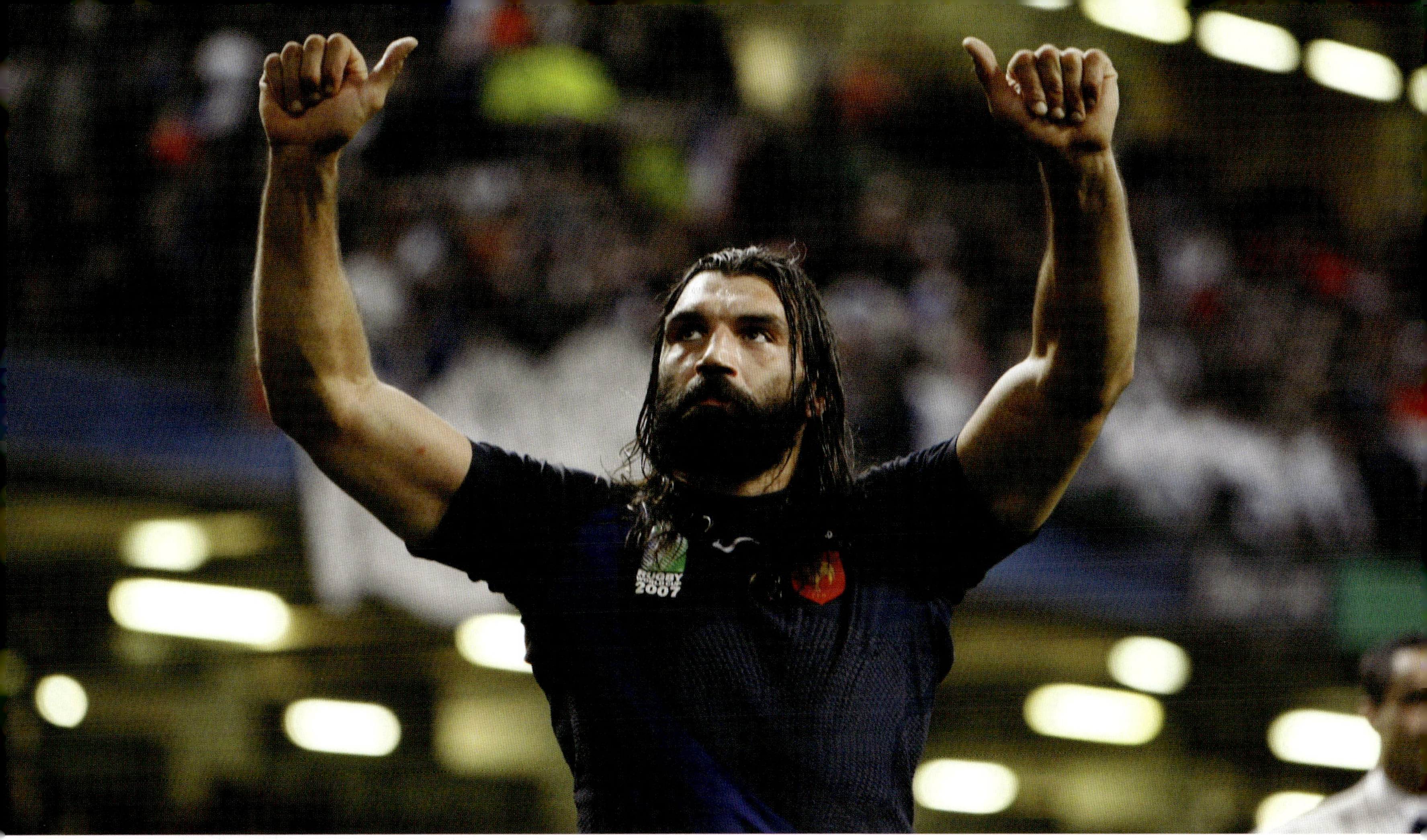
RUGBY
2007

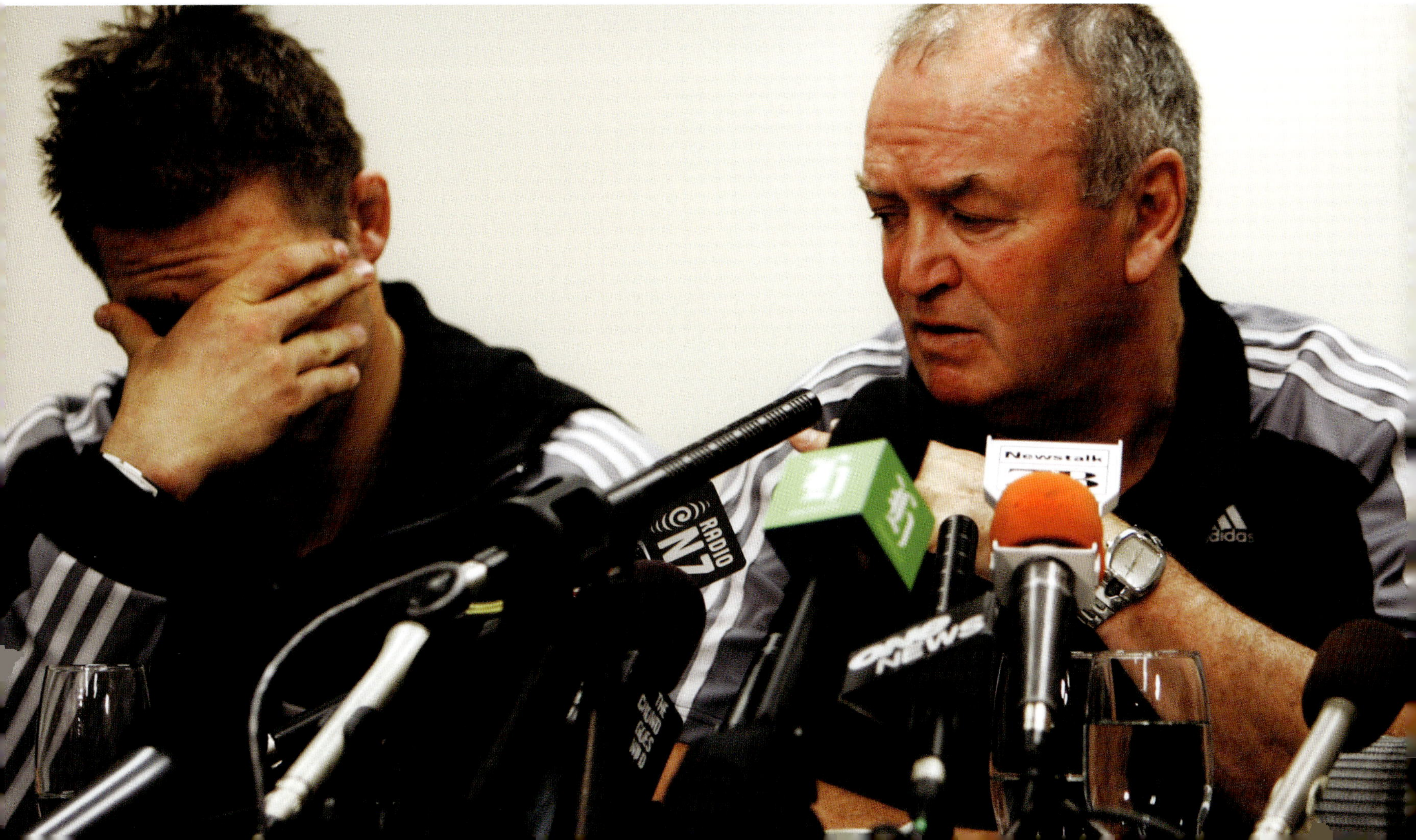
Newstalk
RADIO
adidas
NEWS

a very entertaining test match. But, of course, the perception is that it all came down to a 60-metre breakout, started by Damian Traille, taken on by Freddie Michalak and finished by Yanick Jauzion scoring the match-winner. The only problem being, of course, that there was a massive forward pass from Traille that was missed by referee Wayne Barnes.

But that's not why the All Blacks lost. While they played well, the truth is that on that day in Cardiff they simply ran into a French team that played better. Final score: 20–18 and the All Blacks were on their way home again.

'The feeling in the shed is like no-man's land,' said All Blacks hooker Anton Oliver in his biography. 'There's a sort of desolate decay and—I don't want to dramatise it—the smell of death.'

If it seems a bit over the top, the shock of the loss was an incredibly large one for New Zealand. Weeks of angst and soul-searching turned into months, which turned into years. The general feeling was 'how could this have happened again?' However, this result didn't cost the coach his job. Graham Henry was back in charge of the All Blacks by the time the 2011 tournament rolled around, but it hadn't been a smooth ride. His main challenger for the job was Robbie Deans, and the passing over of the Cantabrian saw him cross the Tasman to coach the Wallabies. Deans' first act in charge was to thoroughly defeat the All Blacks in Sydney in 2008, but since then the All Blacks have had the wood on the Wallabies in Bledisloe Cup games.

While the Bledisloe remained safely in the All Blacks' possession, the rest of the road to the World Cup was a tricky one. Three losses to the Springboks in 2009—the first time that had ever happened to one single team since 1998. The 2011 lead-in season was a patchy one too, with losses to the Wallabies and Springboks again. Plus there was the almost unbearable pressure that came with both hosting and trying to win the World Cup. Auckland city had been given a much-needed makeover for the hordes of international fans that were to arrive, but there was a definite corner-cutting feel to some of it. Instead of taking the opportunity to build a new stadium, Eden Park was fitted with scaffolding stands to bump up capacity. Instead of further developing the public transport system, fans were encouraged to walk up to four kilometres from the city to the stadium. The opening match between the All Blacks and Tonga gridlocked the city for an entire night because nobody considered the possibility that Auckland's entire Tongan community would flood the CBD to watch the game on screens set up for the public.

However, despite those shortcomings, the 2011 World Cup could easily be considered a success before the final had even kicked off. New Zealand truly had become the 'Stadium of Four Million' that had been touted by organisers in the lead-up, cementing rugby's status as the national obsession at the time. It was hard for even the most un-sports-minded citizen not to get caught up in the wave of hysteria, as the All Blacks seemed finally on track to break the curse that had kept them from the game's ultimate prize.

So the stage was set. It was the latest in the year that the All Blacks had ever played on home soil, with the temperature in Auckland starting to climb into the hot and humid summers it's known for. The team bus snaked its way through the traffic from the hotel, past footpaths jammed with supporters waving and cheering. On board was Stephen Donald, the late replacement for Slade who would presumably sit on the bench for the entire game and perhaps become an oddity in the official list of World Cup winners. The year before, Donald had been blamed for a shock loss to the Wallabies in Hong Kong of all places, making him about as popular as Wayne Barnes outside of his

Waikato province. He would have been hoping it'd be a straightforward win, like the 37–17 trouncing in the two sides' pool game a month beforehand. In fact, all of the All Blacks would have been thinking the same, but they were wrong.

IT WAS CRISP AND cool by the time the All Blacks and France strode onto Eden Park in October 2011, led by their respective captains. Across the country, pubs, clubs, living rooms and outdoor public viewing areas in the main centres were packed. Down in Christchurch, watching it on TV was as close as they were ever going to get to the tournament. It was only seven months on from the earthquake that killed 185 people and destroyed Lancaster Park. The teams lined up facing the southern stand, full of dignitaries and fans, knowing full well that this was it. The time had arrived for rugby's ultimate showdown. 'La Marseillaise' rang out from the mouths of the French: *formez vos bataillons . . . marchons, marchons—form your battalions . . . march on, march on.*

Maybe it was that penultimate line of the goosebump-raising French national hymn that inspired what happened next. The All Blacks formed up on the eastern side of halfway for the haka, the French on the other side in their white tracksuits, under which they had white jerseys. Dusautoir had won the right to choose what jersey they wore earlier in the week—as a sporting gesture, he opted for the All Blacks to retain the most famous colour in the game for their team's biggest moment. World Rugby had introduced a rule since their 2007 quarter-final encounter that opposition teams had to stay on their own 10-metre line, which the French did in an arrowhead formation. They then linked hands as Piri Weepu began 'Kapa O Pango'. As the All Blacks

Below France's head coach Marc Lièvremont. FRANCOIS GUILLOT/AFP VIA GETTY IMAGES

Though he had effectively been fired by his own staff weeks before the 2011 final, French coach Marc Lièvremont had one final role to play on the grandest stage of all. With five minutes to go, he sent on substitute Jean-Marc Doussain at halfback. Doussain's only contribution was to knock the ball on and hand possession back to the All Blacks, which they didn't relinquish for the rest of the game. Lièvremont's move meant that Doussain is the only player ever to make his test debut in a World Cup final, and was his last official decision before returning to France and officially losing his job as national team coach.

A bird's-eye view of the haka ahead of the 2011 World Cup final. HANNAH PETERS/GETTY IMAGES

Opposite The French team advance in formation.
HANNAH PETERS/GETTY IMAGES

rose for the first time, drawing the mana from their home ground and slapping their forearms, Dusautoir pulled his battalion forward. They were not going to be intimidated tonight.

They moved to halfway. Then stepped over, into enemy territory. The All Blacks rose furiously and thrust their arms forward and back, but the French kept coming. All the way, till they were about five metres from the All Blacks formation, as the crowd roared to both the haka and the response. While it would have been preferable for many in attendance that this final would turn out to be a one-sided All Blacks win, the French show of defiance stirred up the passion of the home crowd too.

It proved to be a prophetic gesture. The 2011 Rugby World Cup final turned out to be trench warfare of the most brutal order, paying more tribute to the battlefields of almost a century before than to the free-flowing style of rugby that both teams had built their reputations on. Scrum, lineout, kick, repeat. One-off runners. Penalties. The only score of the first half came from a brilliant piece of espionage on the French lineout tactics, when Tony Woodcock went almost untouched through a yawning gap five metres out from the line. It was highly ironic that such a conservative game had been broken open by a slick bit of skill, but there it was: 5–0 to the All Blacks after 40 minutes of otherwise archaic and confrontational rugby.

Then came Donald's famous moment. Cruden was down injured, so the vilified Waikato man ran on in his ill-fitting number 21 jersey. France were penalised 30 metres out, and with one kick, Donald went from zero to World Cup hero. The scoreboard ticked over to 8–0 as he chugged back to halfway, tugging down the jersey that had presumably been tailored for Cruden. The way this game was going, that might be all the All Blacks would need.

The hero of four years prior, after scoring a crucial try against the All Blacks in Cardiff, Dusautoir was about to prove the great leader by example again. Here he was, all 100 kilograms and six foot two of him, now officially captaining his country in a World Cup final. Only moments after Donald's kick, the French grabbed back possession and set up camp in the All Blacks' 22.

The French backline drifted towards the right-hand touchline but Dusautoir saw his gap and ran straight ahead in midfield. Aurélien Rougerie popped him a perfect short ball and the French captain brushed off Ma'a Nonu—a man not known for missing too many tackles—before dotting down next to the post. The All Blacks' lead had been cut to one point, and a nation held its collective breath during what transpired over the course of the next half-hour.

As it turned out, it was an awful lot of tackling. Both sides realised that the slightest slip-up could cost them the World Cup, so reduced an already conservative game plan to complete shutdown. For the most part, the game resembled a pre-war (the first one) rugby league match, with the crowd slowly cottoning on to the idea that the All Blacks were happy enough with their points tally and were going to make every single person in New Zealand live or die on every possession they had. François Trinh-Duc, another man with his heritage rooted in France's colonial past (his grandfather came from what is now Vietnam), missed a shot from halfway that would have put France in the lead after 65 minutes.

That, unbelievably, was as close as either team got to scoring until the final whistle. When it came, the All Blacks had ground away with the ball for the better part of 10 minutes. Replacement halfback Andy Ellis had the honour of punting the ball high into the grandstand to signal the end—now New Zealand could open its eyes, because there would be a plethora of images that would never be forgotten. Donald laughing as he realised what he'd just done, McCaw hoisting the trophy above his head, thousands dancing in the streets of Auckland as a victory parade triumphantly made its way up Queen Street.

But the All Blacks weren't the only heroes to leave Eden Park that night. Thierry Dusautoir and his French side had come from nowhere to be challenging for the sport's biggest prize and barely anyone had given them a chance. They contested the final in a way only the French possibly could, without a coach (the players refused to shake Lièvremont's hand at the end, although it's debatable whether he wanted to do so anyway), having lost to a minnow team, and relying on the ineptitude of others along the way. Once they got there, their captain led from the front with a performance that saw him win man of the match despite being on the losing team.

That epic performance, of both Dusautoir and his side, began with them confronting the haka. A few years later, when reflecting on the arrowhead formation that drew such a vocal response from the 61,079 at Eden Park, Dusautoir said that it meant: 'We are ready for you. Maybe you are going to win, but you're going to have a hard day.'

For the All Blacks, and indeed the entire nation, that's *exactly* what it was.

This page What might have been: Thierry Dusautoir walks past the World Cup on the way to collect his second-place medal. TIM CLAYTON/CORBIS VIA GETTY IMAGES

Opposite The moment all of New Zealand had been waiting for. DAVID DAVIES/PA IMAGES VIA GETTY IMAGES

THE GREAT HAKA REVIVAL

Opposite Steve McDowall leads the haka in Nantes, France, in 1990. SIMON BRUTY/ALLSPORT

18 November 1989
Lansdowne Road, Dublin

All Blacks 23
(John Gallagher, Wayne Shelford, Terry Wright tries; Grant Fox 3 pen, con)

Ireland 6
(Brian Smith 2 pen)

All Blacks	Ireland
15 John Gallagher	15 Philip Rainey
14 Craig Innes	14 Kenneth Hooks
13 Joe Stanley	13 Brendan Mullin
12 John Schuster	12 David Irwin
11 Terry Wright	11 Keith Crossan
10 Grant Fox	10 Brian Smith
9 Graeme Bachop	9 Fergus Aherne
8 Wayne Shelford (c)	8 Noel Mannion
7 Mike Brewer	7 Pat O'Hara
6 Andy Earl	6 Phillip Matthews
5 Gary Whetton	5 Willie Anderson (c)
4 Murray Pierce	4 Donal Lenihan
3 Richard Loe	3 James McCoy
2 Sean Fitzpatrick	2 Steve Smith
1 Steve McDowall	1 Nick Popplewell

Reserves

16 Bruce Deans	16 Des Fitzgerald
17 Walter Little	17 Phil Danaher
18 Matthew Ridge	18 Ralph Keyes
19 Warren Gatland	19 Michael Bradley
20 Graham Purvis	20 Paul Collins
21 Zinzan Brooke	21 Terry Kingston

Wayne 'Buck' Shelford during a match against Newport on the 1989 tour.
RUSSELL CHEYNE/GETTY IMAGES

'He changed it overnight. He captured not just Māori, but the country's imagination.'
—WILLIE JACKSON, MĀORI BROADCASTER AND POLITICIAN

RUGBY FAN OR NOT, ask anyone around the world what they know about New Zealand and often the first words you hear out of their mouth are the All Blacks and the haka. It's a simple exercise which shows that the haka has transcended rugby and is now one of New Zealand's key markers on the world stage. While the haka, the All Blacks and New Zealand are all indelibly linked, it could have been very different if not for the influence of Buck Shelford in the 1980s.

'The haka basically didn't happen. It was a tame jig at best,' Shelford explained to *Rugby World*'s Sam Tremlett. 'Many players didn't enjoy it—they were either embarrassed or didn't feel any connection to it. There was plenty of discussion about whether we should bother at all.'

Despite being an important part of New Zealand rugby tradition for almost 100 years, the place of the haka inside the All Blacks was at a crossroads when Shelford made the All Blacks in 1985. It was performed sporadically and was a bubblegum version of what you see today—rushed, unchoreographed and delivered with little meaning behind it.

> A few of the guys asked me and Hika Reid what we thought. Our response was that the haka should only be done if everyone would do it without inhibition and with understanding of the culture and history behind it. We needed 100 per cent buy-in from everyone—the New Zealand union, the players, the Pākehā guys in the All Blacks, everyone. And if we were going to do it, we were going to do it well, and that meant practising it until we were perfect, just as we did with lineouts and scrums. It had to mean something special. It had to represent us to the world.

Starting with the All Blacks tour to Argentina in 1985, Shelford and Reid set about not just teaching the All Blacks the correct way to haka, but also the concept of tikanga.

'It was about doing it right and not disrespecting our people back home—our tangata whenua,' said Shelford.

Derived from the Māori word 'tika', meaning right or correct, tikanga is a social construct central to Māori people. Forged over many generations, tikanga describes a set of protocols, behaviours and beliefs that are culturally proper and appropriate. Simply put, tikanga could be referred to as the 'Māori way of doing things'. Shelford and Reid were the perfect people to introduce this concept to the All Blacks. Born

Opposite Shelford leads the haka before the All Blacks tour match against Swansea. RUSSELL CHEYNE/GETTY IMAGES

and raised in the Māori heartland of Rotorua, they had been immersed in kapa haka and Māori culture their entire lives. They quickly built their teammates' understanding of tikanga and what it meant to perform the haka. 'If we're going to do it, we are going to teach it properly, because I don't want to be disrespectful to our tīpuna [ancestors] and be an embarrassment on TV all over the world,' Shelford said.

It didn't take long for people outside the All Blacks to notice Shelford and Reid's influence. 'And then all of a sudden this Buck Shelford came along and introduced rugby to mana Māori,' broadcaster Willie Jackson said. 'He changed it overnight. He captured not just Māori, but the country's imagination.' New Zealand comedian Mike King had an even more candid take on the sudden change. 'They took it from a whole lot of white guys dancing at a disco and turned it into what it should be.'

The All Blacks' revitalised haka engendered such a sense of national pride that it was performed at home for the 1987 Rugby World Cup, having rarely been seen on home soil. After the All Blacks' breakthrough win in the tournament, it has been a part of every one of their test matches since.

By the time of the All Blacks tour of Canada and Europe in 1989, the haka was receiving widespread acclaim and opposition teams began to think about how they would face up to the challenge. In the case of Newport RFC, it was more a matter of how they would avoid the haka, as they remained in a huddle on their own tryline instead of coming up to halfway to face the challenge. With no International Rugby Football Board (now World Rugby) protocols in place about where to stand in 1989, Shelford famously led the All Blacks all the way downfield to perform 'Ka Mate' on the Newport tryline. It was a strong statement that the haka commanded respect and it was no coincidence that the All Blacks went on to record their highest score of the 14-match tour with a 54–9 victory.

Less than two weeks later, the All Blacks faced a different proposition from Irish powerhouse Munster in Limerick. The Munster side came up to halfway and linked arms to face the challenge from Shelford and the All Blacks head on. Although eventually losing 31–9, it was a stark contrast to Newport's timid response and laid the platform for the final test of the tour, and last major international match of the 1980s, between the All Blacks and Ireland at Lansdowne Road.

The All Blacks were the reigning Rugby World Cup champions and had previously met Ireland eight times in Dublin for seven hard-fought wins and one draw since their first clash in 1905. The last meeting between the two old foes was in 1978 and Lansdowne Road was at fever pitch for the resumption of the rivalry. As the All Blacks lined up to perform the haka, Ireland linked arms and marched up to halfway, led by captain Willie Anderson. This was holy ground for Irish rugby, and it was clear they weren't going to roll over. In his 2016 book, *Donal Lenihan: My Life in Rugby*, Irish lock Lenihan described what happened next:

Opposite top Ireland's Willie Anderson knows he's in a battle. BOB THOMAS SPORTS PHOTOGRAPHY VIA GETTY IMAGES

Opposite below The 1987 World Cup semi-final between the All Blacks and Wales in Brisbane, Australia. RUSSELL CHEYNE/ ALLSPORT

I was halfway down the line to the left of Willie, who was standing right in the middle with seven men either side of him, when suddenly, and without any warning to the rest of us, he started advancing on the New Zealand players. Along with everyone else, I was looking across the line wondering, what the f**k is going on here? That's why you started to see this V forming with Willie as the arrowhead, leading the charge. It ended up with him practically in Shelford's face as the Lansdowne Road crowd went ballistic in response.

The performance concluded with the opposing captains just centimetres away from each other, and some members of the All Blacks unable to complete their trademark haka-ending leap.

'You have to not only match them in the haka, you have to go toe to toe the whole way,' said Willie Anderson. 'And the atmosphere was . . . if you could have bottled it, you would have made a fortune.' The red-hot Lansdowne Road atmosphere didn't abate during a pulsating contest that saw the All Blacks run out victorious 23–6 on the back of tries to Shelford, John Gallagher and Terry Wright. 'I always said that we won the dance but lost the match,' Anderson said.

While that haka will go down in history as a turning point of how teams face the All Blacks' challenge, so too will a peculiar incident during the match where a Grant Fox try was overturned by the intervention of a ball boy. In the seventieth minute, and with the All Blacks leading by just 13–6, Grant Fox thought he had his first test try when he outflanked the Irish defence down the short side. But on the opposite side of the field, a touch judge remained unmoved with his flag up in the air for an All Blacks' indiscretion three minutes earlier. With no television match official (TMO) available in 1989, and the howls of the home crowd going unheard by referee Sandy McNeill, a 13-year-old ball boy ran across the field to inform the referee and ensure that the try was overturned. It was a big moment in the game, and one that could have been even more controversial if it hadn't been for the All Blacks' strong finish to the match.

Despite their fierce confrontation during the haka, opposing captains Wayne Shelford and Willie Anderson paid respect to each other after the final whistle. 'Willie's response was the way to do it,' said Shelford. 'After all, New Zealand has never won a game because of the haka. We've won because we've played better rugby across 80 minutes.'

KIERAN READ TAKES THE LEAD

Opposite Kieran Read leads his players as they perform the haka prior to the 2019 Rugby World Cup bronze-final match between New Zealand and Wales. DAN MULLAN/GETTY IMAGES

24 November 2018
Stadio Olimpico, Rome

All Blacks 66
(Jordie Barrett 4, Damian McKenzie 3, Beauden Barrett, Ngani Laumape, TJ Perenara tries; Beauden Barrett 5 con, Richie Mo'unga 3 con)

Italy 3
(Tommaso Allan pen)

All Blacks	**Italy**
15 Damian McKenzie	15 Jayden Hayward
14 Jordie Barrett	14 Tommaso Benvenuti
13 Anton Lienert-Brown	13 Michele Campagnaro
12 Ngani Laumape	12 Tommaso Castello
11 Waisake Naholo	11 Luca Sperandio
10 Beauden Barrett	10 Tommaso Allan
9 TJ Perenara	9 Tito Tebaldi
8 Kieran Read (c)	8 Braam Steyn
7 Ardie Savea	7 Jake Polledri
6 Vaea Fifita	6 Sebastian Negri da Ollegio
5 Scott Barrett	5 Dean Budd
4 Patrick Tuipulotu	4 Alessandro Zanni
3 Nepo Laulala	3 Simone Ferrari
2 Dane Coles	2 Leonardo Ghiraldini (c)
1 Ofa Tuungafasi	1 Andrea Lovotti

Reserves	**Reserves**
16 Nathan Harris	16 Luca Bigi
17 Karl Tu'inukuafe	17 Cherif Traore
18 Angus Ta'avao	18 Tiziano Pasquali
19 Brodie Retallick	19 Marco Fuser
20 Dalton Papali'i	20 Johan Meyer
21 Te Toiroa Tahuriorangi	21 Guglielmo Pallazzani
22 Richie Mo'unga	22 Luca Morisi
23 Rieko Ioane	23 Edoardo Padovani

Read leads the haka for the first time in November 2018. FILIPPO MONTEFORTE/ AFP VIA GETTY IMAGES

'It's a tremendous honour to lead it, and whilst it's a tremendous honour, it's also a tremendous responsibility because you're not only representing the All Blacks, you're representing the iwi which belongs to that haka, and all of our Māori brothers and sisters.'

—KIERAN READ, ALL BLACKS CAPTAIN

THINGS WEREN'T LOOKING GOOD on the Monday after the All Blacks played Ireland in November of 2018. That test had been hyped up all year, as it was the chance for a bit of revenge after the shock loss to the Irish in Chicago in 2016. This time, though, the two sides had met in Dublin in the penultimate test of what was a very long season for the All Blacks. Even more so, it was a year out from the World Cup, so the players and staff knew full well that as soon as they were back in New Zealand, they'd have to immediately start thinking about their trip to Japan. On the one hand, the test against Ireland meant everything in terms of World Cup build-up because by the end of 2018 the Irish were arguably the best side in the world. On the other, it meant nothing because the All Blacks were finishing their season while the Irish were just starting theirs.

But then the All Blacks went and lost. Not in typical All Blacks fashion, mind you. Every loss this century up until the test in Dublin had been a high-scoring affair, with a large aggregate of points and tries. You have to go back to 1999 to find a defeat where they were kept to under 15 points: a record 28–7 loss to the Wallabies in Sydney. Indeed, the breakthrough win that Ireland had achieved in Chicago was a shootout scoreline that would've looked right at home in the early years of Super Rugby: 40–29 after the Irish had been up 30–3 at one stage; they had to fight off an All Blacks comeback that saw Read's men surge to within a point of the lead for a time.

The week before Dublin had been a grind of a game at Twickenham, against England. This one went the way that physical battles against the All Blacks usually go—a massive second-half arm wrestle that saw the All Blacks win 16–15. The result basically saved Eddie Jones' job and set them up for a rematch at the World Cup in a year's time. (You can read about what happened before that particular match in another chapter.)

So it was fair to say the resulting 16–9 loss to Ireland in front of a packed Aviva Stadium came as a bit of a shock. There was only one try in the game, which turned out to be the difference between the two sides. It was scored in the second half by winger Jacob Stockdale, off a move that Irish coach Joe Schmidt had arguably copied from one the All Blacks had pulled off three weeks previously against the Wallabies in Tokyo—a quick change of direction from a set-piece move on halfway that gave Stockdale enough room to bust down the blind side, chip ahead and score.

Left in his wake, a forlorn sight for New Zealanders: Kieran Read, All Blacks captain, on his back 50 metres away and struggling to get

up. He'd been dropped out of the lineout that had led to the try, landing heavily and doing a bit of damage. The gap he left was all that Stockdale had needed. In a match of inches, Read's mishap was, at first glance, to prove the winning and losing of the game. But the truth is, he was far from alone. All the senior All Blacks had played their most ineffectual rugby of the entire season that night, with passes dropped, tackles missed and penalties given away. The post-match press conference was one of pure public relations by coach Steve Hansen, because he knew that there was no excuse for such a piss-poor performance. It was no one's fault but their own, and full credit should go to Schmidt and the Irish. Hansen did drop one telling remark about the Irish now being the best team in the world, and how it was up to them to prove that they deserved that spot.

Two days later, the All Blacks were in Rome.

As well as the typically brutal post-match analysis from opinion writers back in New Zealand that usually follows a test loss, there was a degree of unprecedented criticism reserved especially for Read. It was an odd scenario, and a somewhat new one for a lot of All Blacks fans. Read's predecessor, the incomparable Richie McCaw, somehow never seemed to have a bad game. Neither did the man he took over from, Tana Umaga. You have to go all the way back to Reuben Thorne to find a man in charge of the All Blacks that faced constant scrutiny over his actual on-field deeds. That was a long, long time ago—after all, by 2018 the All Blacks were back-to-back world champions and were seemingly well on track to make that three in a row.

Read was renowned as a freakishly talented number 8, possessed of some of the most brilliant on-field awareness anyone had ever seen, but

Opposite Kieran Read leads the haka during pool play at the 2019 Rugby World Cup. CRAIG MERCER/MB MEDIA/GETTY IMAGES

there had been arguments that he might be too old to be carrying a captain's workload when the World Cup rolled around. The flat performance against the Irish turned up the volume on those keen to grab the public's attention, making the previously unthinkable prospect of the All Blacks captain being replaced within a year of the World Cup a concerning possibility.

So, Monday in Rome was a time to address that insinuation. In a heated press conference, Hansen took the bull by the horns and left everyone in no doubt about where he stood. Read was his captain and, yes, he'd played below his best on the weekend but that was over and done.

'First of all, his back was a career-ending possibility so he had to deal with that. He's had some lessons on the track as a leader and he's come through that fine. He's got all the respect in the world from the team,' Hansen fired at the media gathered at the All Blacks' hotel.

> He knocked the ball on, which was pretty costly. He knows that and he's bitterly disappointed about that but that's rugby. Sometimes that happens. He'd take that opportunity 99 times out of 100. Saturday was the one time. We all understand that if you're in the All Blacks environment you're going to be scrutinised and you'll have your turn in the sun but you'll also have your turn in the rain and people are going to have plenty to say. You've just got to be strong enough to believe in who you are. He's well supported so his position is not under threat.

Hansen then delivered a withering attack on journalists back in New Zealand who were daring to question his captain. It left everyone in the conference room in the Roman hotel very clear as to who would be leading out the All Blacks at the World Cup. But what happened on the day of the actual test match would eradicate any lingering doubts on that score anyway.

STADIO OLIMPICO SITS ON the western bank of the river Tiber. When you approach up the Viale dei Gladiatori from the city end, you must walk past a line of statues of classical-period athletes. They are perfectly formed human figures, bodies frozen in the precise moment of sporting endeavour. In keeping with the style of the traditional marble statue, the shot putters, sprinters, hammer and javelin throwers are completely naked. While there is no rugby player statue, clothed or otherwise, the local sponsors of the test match between Italy and the All Blacks had managed to put up some inflatable players around 10 feet high that bobbed about in the gentle breeze as the large crowd walked up to the stadium gates.

There were 57,000 in to watch the All Blacks' last match of the tour—which is who the vast majority were there to see, because the Italians' test record in 2018 barely made them worth the price of entrance. It didn't matter that the world champions had just been knocked off their perch by Ireland. This was a visceral reminder that the All Blacks are the only game in rugby-town when it comes to pulling a crowd—even attracting curious

neutrals who would otherwise have no interest in 30 men assaulting each other over the possession of a synthetic ball.

Of course, there was something else they were here to see other than what would end up being a terrifically entertaining, but one-sided, victory to the All Blacks. The Romans in attendance, piled up in the Curva Nord and Sud sections usually inhabited by local Roma and Lazio football fans, wanted to see the haka. For them, its every rendition signifies what rugby is. Today they were going to see one that symbolised just what the All Blacks captaincy means.

It was fitting that this display of unity took place at Stadio Olimpico. Even though the test result was a foregone conclusion, it's a special venue for any New Zealand sports fan. It was here in 1960 that we truly punched above our weight at the Olympic Games, when Murray Halberg and Peter Snell won gold medals within an hour of one another. The track they ran on has been relaid since then, but still rings the field where the two teams walked on to do battle on that late-November afternoon in the Eternal City. For the All Blacks it was the last match of the year, and you got the feeling that most of them were pretty happy about that. The loss to Ireland sat alongside a home defeat to the Springboks earlier in the season, with their not exactly dominant form on the last stretch giving the press more to chew on than just Read's performance. There was talk that either the team was running on fumes, or they were deliberately holding back their main game plan till next season. Or both.

But the job had to be done. Italy have never beaten the All Blacks, and most likely never will, so Hansen changed up his starting XV to give some of the wider squad a run. Kieran Read still led the team out on Stadio Olimpico, and lined up on halfway for the national anthem. Then the phones came out.

All across the stadium, from top to bottom, the crowd hushed as the All Blacks formed up the niho (haka formation). But unlike every other test in 2018, TJ Perenara wasn't lurking behind the second row to call the team to order. Instead, it was Read. While Hansen's words earlier in the week were strong, this symbolic gesture said it all. 'Ka mate! Ka mate!' the captain's voice rang out as kaea [leader]. The All Blacks responded, thundered out the traditional challenge, and gave the crowd the pictures and videos they wanted. The stands erupted with applause at the end, while up in the media box, heads from the locals quickly turned up to the scattering of New Zealand journalists who had made the trip to Europe.

'Why does . . . uhhhh . . . Key-ron lead the haka?'

'Is this not the . . . job of a Māori player?'

'Were you to know this was to happen today?'

All the New Zealanders could do was shrug. The only thing they knew about the team protocols of the haka was that they didn't really know anything at all; it's just as tightly guarded as the plays they run off set piece. No one is across how often the All Blacks practise it, which one they'll perform, or who exactly will lead it. We can only make educated guesses.

The game itself went exactly the way everyone thought it would. By full-time, the scoreline read 66–3 against the hapless Italians, with Jordie Barrett claiming four tries and Damian McKenzie three. The first of Barrett's tries was set up by a kick across field by his brother Beauden (which makes sense); the last was from a kick across field by replacement hooker Nathan Harris (which doesn't). Of course, all anyone wanted to know afterwards was why Read had taken it upon himself to lead the haka.

In typical All Blacks fashion, it was dealt with by denial first up. This wasn't something that the team was doing in response to the critique of their captain during the week.

'No. You don't just rock up and lead the haka, it takes a lot of preparation,' said Hansen in the huge Stadio Olimpico media room. 'To be able to lead it well, it's probably something you would put half a year, or a whole year, of work into.'

It seemed a little far-fetched. Why would a big moment like this end up happening in the last test of the year at 3am New Zealand time? In Read's 2019 biography, *Straight 8*, he says:

> It was an enormous honour, one that was widely depicted as an act of defiance on my part. That couldn't be further from the truth. I had a team that was hurting, one that needed to make one final push for the year. I wasn't trying to prove anything to the public. I was standing in front of my men and leading them.

Opposite The pressure: Read is interrogated by the press. MATT BROWNE/SPORTSFILE VIA GETTY IMAGES

Opposite top Kieran Read celebrates following the big win in Rome. PHIL WALTER/GETTY IMAGES

Opposite below Guglielmo Palazzani swaps jerseys with TJ Perenara after the match. PHIL WALTER/GETTY IMAGES

Whatever the case, it wasn't as serious as the news that Read's back injury wasn't caused against Ireland—it was one that he'd been carrying for a while. The All Blacks captain headed into the off-season and a lengthy break in preparation for the World Cup, which would be his last campaign in the All Blacks jersey. There was time for him to be leading the haka again before he'd hang that jersey up for good, though.

KIERAN READ AND TJ PERENARA have a special relationship as senior men in the All Blacks. Together, they would spring another surprise once the World Cup eventually rolled around and the team found themselves out on the turf of Yokohama International Stadium. Everything feels a little different at a World Cup: the teams wear special jerseys, there's just that much more pomp and ceremony, and the crowd for the game between the All Blacks and the Springboks was mostly made up of local Japanese fans eager to see another instalment of rugby's greatest rivalry. So it made sense that the All Blacks conspired to make the haka that night a special one too.

They performed 'Kapa O Pango', as they usually do against opponents of great stature. However, when the All Blacks formed up in the niho, its point was missing. Instead of Perenara being the sole kaea, Read stood beside him and called out the commands for the team to drop to one knee and prepare to face their enemy.

Taringa whakarongo!
Kia rite! Kia rite! Kia mau!
Hī!
Kia whakawhenua au i ahau!
Hī, auē! Hī!

The players around him sank to the earth, left palms gripping their right forearms. The All Blacks captain strode forward dramatically to join them at the head of the niho, and Perenara then took the lead.

Ko Aotearoa, e ngunguru nei!
Hī, au! Au! Auē, hā! Hī!

Just as in Rome the year before, the media boxes were abuzz.

After what the All Blacks had gone through in the lead-up to the World Cup, though, it wasn't surprising that Read had decided to make such a statement. Things hadn't exactly gone to plan for the side, who started with a scratchy win over Argentina in Buenos Aires, managed a draw with the Springboks in Wellington, then were given a record hiding by the Wallabies in Perth. The pressure had come on big-time when they arrived in Auckland for the return Bledisloe Cup match, with a gigantic media contingent clawing for answers at the slew of press conferences and the traditional Friday captain's run.

Things hadn't gone smoothly in the lead-up to previous World Cups either, but that didn't stop a fair amount of panic setting in among All Blacks fans over how the team was shaping up to defend

The haka before the bronze final was the last one that Read would lead for the All Blacks. LYNNE CAMERON/ GETTY IMAGES

their title. Some of that anxiety was assuaged with an assured win and retention of the Bledisloe that weekend. However, everybody knew that the challenge from the rest of the rugby world would be stiffer than ever once the All Blacks reached Japan.

This wasn't the first time a Pākehā had led the haka. Richie McCaw took it upon himself to lead the side in 2013 and 2015, but when Read stepped up it seemed to be in direct response to his form. Perenara, for his part, said that it was heartening to see his Pākehā captain go through a te reo Māori journey of this nature.

'What I've been saying to him is he is the leader of our group and when he steps up and leads haka, I think it gives our team mana,' said the halfback the week after the All Blacks' eventual win over the Springboks in Yokohama. 'Even for Māori back home to see non-Māori go through the processes to learn why he's leading haka, pronouncing the words the right way, and doing it the way he's performed it, that's special to me, not even as a rugby player or a teammate, but as a Māori.'

In the end, sadly, the 2019 World Cup just wasn't to be for the All Blacks. But the haka that was performed to open the tournament will live long in the memory of those who were there to witness it. Any time there is a slight change to proceedings, or a cultural shift like a Pākehā becoming more involved like Kieran Read did, it generates an immense amount of interest from the sporting media.

It is, in Read's own words, 'an honour'.

KIERAN READ TAKES THE LEAD / 105

THE PRODIGAL SON

Opposite Quade Cooper of the Wallabies jostles with All Blacks captain Richie McCaw during the final Tri Nations test of 2011.
PHIL WALTER/GETTY IMAGES

27 August 2011
Suncorp Stadium, Brisbane

All Blacks 20
(Conrad Smith, Ma'a Nonu tries;
Dan Carter 2 pen, 2 con)

Wallabies 25
(Will Genia, Radike Samo, Kurtley Beale tries;
Quade Cooper 2 pen, 2 con)

All Blacks	**Wallabies**
15 Mils Muliaina	15 Kurtley Beale
14 Cory Jane	14 Adam Ashley-Cooper
13 Conrad Smith	13 Anthony Fainga'a
12 Ma'a Nonu	12 Pat McCabe
11 Zac Guildford	11 Digby Ioane
10 Dan Carter	10 Quade Cooper
9 Piri Weepu	9 Will Genia
8 Kieran Read	8 Radike Samo
7 Richie McCaw (c)	7 David Pocock
6 Adam Thomson	6 Rocky Elsom
5 Samuel Whitelock	5 James Horwill (c)
4 Brad Thorn	4 Dan Vickerman
3 Owen Franks	3 Ben Alexander
2 Keven Mealamu	2 Stephen Moore
1 Tony Woodcock	1 Sekope Kepu

Reserves | **Reserves**

16 Andrew Hore	16 Saia Fainga'a
17 John Afoa	17 Salesi Ma'afu
18 Ali Williams	18 Rob Simmons
19 Victor Vito	19 Ben McCalman
20 Andy Ellis	20 Scott Higginbotham
21 Colin Slade	21 Luke Burgess
22 Isaia Toeava	22 Rob Horne

Both the Bledisloe Cup (left) and the Tri Nations Trophy were on the line at Suncorp Stadium on 27 August 2011. CAMERON SPENCER/GETTY IMAGES

'You do get a bit of mixed emotions [facing up to the haka] because you just feel that fire and passion build up and I think I just try and feed off that.'

—QUADE COOPER, WALLABIES
NEW ZEALAND-BORN PLAYMAKER

IN 2011, NO ONE drew more negative headlines, irate talkback callers or booing fans in New Zealand than Wallabies playmaker Quade Cooper.

Born in the Waikato town of Tokoroa, Cooper moved to Australia at the age of 13 and quickly became a schoolboy star in Brisbane. Blessed with instinctive running, a booming boot and slick ball skills, Cooper accelerated through the age-grade system before making his Super Rugby debut for the Reds at just 18 years of age in 2006. A Wallabies test debut came two years later and Cooper's ascension from humble Tokoroa teenager to Australian rugby prodigy was complete.

Despite being regarded as one of the brightest young talents on the world stage, it wasn't until 2010 that Cooper would finally take the field against the country of his birth. With the All Blacks on a 15-test winning streak, and building towards a home Rugby World Cup, Cooper gave New Zealand fans an ominous glimpse of his talent by scoring a crucial try in the Wallabies' 26–24 victory in Hong Kong and engaging in a number of verbal battles with the team in black along the way. Just like that, Quade Cooper had become the biggest threat to the All Blacks' chances of reclaiming the Rugby World Cup in 2011—a trophy they had not held since 1987.

New Zealand fans were rightly worried about Cooper's mercurial talent. He was brash, combative, flamboyant and had a bag of tricks that would make magician David Copperfield proud. To make matters worse for Kiwi fans, he was born in heartland New Zealand. The thought of losing a Rugby World Cup to a Wallabies side with a New Zealand-born playmaker seemed too much for some, judging by talkback callers and website commentators at the time.

If 2010 sowed the seed of this rivalry, 2011 was when it sprouted to uncontrollable levels. In the fifty-fourth minute of the Tri Nations test between the Wallabies and the All Blacks at Suncorp Stadium, Cooper appeared to knee All Blacks captain Richie McCaw square in the face while attempting to stand up from a ruck. It was a sickening connection and one that saw Cooper's future coach Brad Thorn leap to McCaw's defence and pin the Wallabies pivot to the ground. The mêlée was quickly cleared and the Wallabies went on to win 25–20. It marked Australia's first Tri Nations title win since 2001 and put a spoke in the wheel of the All Blacks' Rugby World Cup hopes.

Cooper escaped any sanction, with the SANZAR judiciary commenting that on the 'balance of probability' contact had been accidental. Regardless, the wrath of New Zealand fans was triggered and a collision course was set for the All

Opposite top Tension between Quade Cooper and Richie McCaw in the 2011 World Cup semi-final. TIM CLAYTON/CORBIS VIA GETTY IMAGES

Opposite below Good mates: Quade Cooper (a New Zealander playing for Australia) gets to know Brad Thorn (an Australian playing for New Zealand). DAVID DAVIES/PA IMAGES VIA GETTY IMAGES

Blacks and Wallabies at the 2011 Rugby World Cup. Speaking on the Ice Project podcast with childhood friend Isaac John, Cooper said that nothing could have prepared him for the reception he received from the home fans at the tournament:

> So I walked into New Zealand for the World Cup, and it was just like, I have never been involved in anything like that. I couldn't go anywhere, I couldn't walk. People were coming up asking for photos and things like this, but as soon as they were away, I was on the team bus and everyone was shouting, with signs, saying 'I hope you break your leg'. Things like that. I went from being well known to the most well known and the most hated. It was crazy. I look back at it now and I think, *I wasn't ready for it.*

By the time the All Blacks and Australia met in the Rugby World Cup semi-final at Eden Park, New Zealand fans had whipped themselves into a frenzy and Cooper was their main target.

The whole nation seemed on edge. The All Blacks had not won the tournament for 24 years, and memories of their semi-final exit to Australia in 2003 and quarter-final flop to France in 2007 were still raw. To make matters worse for nervous All Blacks fans, star first five Dan Carter had limped out of the tournament, with rookie number 10 Aaron Cruden brought in to mark Cooper in the biggest match of his career.

Cooper told TVNZ reporter Carmen Parahi before the match that he wouldn't be fazed by whatever the New Zealand crowd threw at him in the semi-final: 'If they're that worried about me personally that they've got to go to that level of booing and stuff like that then I'll take that as a compliment.' As for facing up to the haka as a player of Māori heritage, Cooper said that it only served to inspire him on the field: 'You do get a bit of mixed emotions because you just feel that fire and passion build up and I think I just try and feed off that.'

Over 60,000 fans packed into Eden Park to generate one of the most electric atmospheres ever experienced in New Zealand sport when the All Blacks and the Wallabies met in the 2011 Rugby World Cup semi-final. Halfback Piri Weepu led the All Blacks in a passionate performance of 'Kapa O Pango' as the Wallabies stood resolute and refused to flinch while the parochial home crowd grew louder throughout the performance.

As the intensity lifted both in the middle of the ground and in the stands, the cameras homed in on Cooper as he stared determinedly back at his opponents laying down the challenge. The crowd reached fever pitch as the All Blacks completed their pre-match ritual and turned around to regroup in a huddle.

Australia didn't budge. They stood shoulder to shoulder, hoping to engage the All Blacks in a staredown that would never eventuate. It was a strong statement from the Wallabies that they were

Below Quade Cooper in happier times at the 2011 Rugby World Cup. GREG WOOD/AFP VIA GETTY IMAGES

Opposite Cooper is tackled by Richard Kahui in the semi-final of the 2011 Rugby World Cup. STU FORSTER/GETTY IMAGES

there to spoil the party and extend the All Blacks' torrid World Cup run for another four years.

Cooper's first touch didn't go according to plan, though. He booted the kick-off into touch on the full to hand the early advantage to the home side. Five minutes later the All Blacks made Australia pay when Israel Dagg sliced through the defence to set up Ma'a Nonu for the first try of the game. It was a telling blow early on and one that Australia never really recovered from. On attack and defence, the All Blacks swarmed, choked and battered Australia. The sight of Jerome Kaino manhandling Wallabies wing Digby Ioane on his way to a certain try was a moment that defined the performance of the All Blacks that night.

Aside from a smartly taken dropped goal in the first half, Cooper was starved of opportunities to showcase his talent and Australia were comfortably dispatched 20–6. It was the All Blacks' first-ever Rugby World Cup win over Australia and set up a final against France. The All Blacks would go on to win the final 8–7 and lift the Webb Ellis Cup for the first time since 1987.

Despite an ongoing battle with New Zealand fans for the remainder of the decade, Cooper did make peace with former All Blacks captain Richie McCaw for the infamous knee incident of 2011, as he explained on the Ice Project podcast.

> A few years later I saw Richie in the airport and I went up to him and said: 'Sorry about that.' It's not that he didn't care or did care, it's just when I said sorry to him, I confronted it. I said: 'I really looked up to you as a kid, you were my idol, everyone in New Zealand loves you, and I loved you. So when I played against you, it was just emotion, passion, all that sort of thing took over.'

Cooper ended his career with 70 tests for the Wallabies and will go down as one of the All Blacks' fiercest and most competitive rivals.

SEVENS WHĀNAU

Opposite Stacey Fluhler of the Black Ferns Sevens scores a try during the Cup final match against Canada.
HAGEN HOPKINS/GETTY IMAGES

26 January 2020
FMG Stadium Waikato, Hamilton

Black Ferns Sevens 24
(Michaela Blyde 2, Niall Williams, Stacey Fluhler tries; Tyla Nathan-Wong 2 con)

All Blacks Sevens 27
(Scott Curry 3, Regan Ware 2 tries; Ngarohi McGarvey-Black con)

Canada 7
(Brittany Benn try; Ghislaine Landry con)

France 5
(Tavite Veredamu try)

Black Ferns Sevens
5 Sarah Hirini (née Goss) (c)
1 Ruby Tui
10 Theresa Fitzpatrick
6 Michaela Blyde
8 Kelly Brazier
7 Tyla Nathan-Wong
3 Stacey Fluhler (née Waaka)

Reserves
9 Gayle Broughton
4 Niall Williams
12 Alena Saili
2 Risi Pouri-Lane
11 Mahina Paul

Canada
4 Kayla Moleschi
7 Karen Paquin
10 Kaili Lukan
8 Bianca Farella
5 Julia Greenshields
9 Ghislaine Landry
2 Brittany Benn

Reserves
11 Elissa Alarie
6 Sara Kaljuvee
1 Charity Williams
3 Caroline Crossley
12 Keyara Wardley

All Blacks Sevens
1 Scott Curry (c)
2 Tim Mikkelson
5 Dylan Collier
10 Kurt Baker
11 Joe Webber
9 Regan Ware
8 Ngarohi McGarvey-Black

Reserves
7 Sam Dickson
12 Sione Molia
3 Tone Ng Shiu
6 Vilimoni Koroi
4 Etene Nanai-Seturo

France
1 Jonathan Laugel
11 Sacha Valleau
3 Tavite Veredamu
4 Terry Bouhraoua
6 Paulin Riva
9 Pierre Mignot
7 Remi Siega

Reserves
10 Jean Pascal Barraque
8 Pierre Gilles Lakafia
5 Stephen Parez
2 Marvin O'Connor
13 Antoine Zeghdar

Sarah Hirini lifts up teammate Michaela Blyde after the team's victory in the women's final. MICHAEL BRADLEY/AFP VIA GETTY IMAGES

'To be standing there in that moment with my jersey on, with my medal on, was unreal. I'd been practising the pūkana for that moment for honestly eight years.'
—RUBY TUI, BLACK FERNS SEVENS

IT HAD BEEN A hot weekend in Hamilton, stinking hot, in fact. The city that everyone loves to call 'the Tron' had turned up the heat for the two days of tournament play in the latest round of the World Sevens Series, so much so that some of the players were saying it was hotter than the Dubai leg. Kurt Baker, veteran of the All Blacks Sevens, said that he could feel the heat bouncing off the lush grass of FMG Stadium Waikato. Around the field that he and his teammates were playing on, the thousands who had flocked to the tournament had been forced to find as much shade as they could throughout the day. It was a relentless heat, the sort that scorched Wellington throughout the first decade of the century back when the tournament was famously held in the nation's capital.

The Sevens being moved to the Waikato signalled a much-needed rebirth of the tournament after Wellington's collective high-nosed sensibilities and bureaucracy saw the two-day party fall out of favour. It also coincided with a kind of rebirth of the Sevens programme, which had to face the fact that things were never going to be the same as they were in the old days in terms of who would be playing for the All Blacks Sevens.

Off the field, while the action had moved to Hamilton, Baker said that it was a pretty similar vibe to the Wellington glory days: 'It's funny, when Fiji or New Zealand would play, everyone comes and watches. The rest of the time they're out the back having a good time, which I think is great. You definitely notice a difference at home—we're pretty lucky that we get this opportunity.'

Mercifully, it had cooled by Sunday evening. It was then that the tournament got the dream result for its organisers, as both the New Zealand men's and women's teams progressed through to their respective finals. This was a big deal—it was the first time the women had been an official part of the New Zealand leg, and the men's first chance to win a title at home in four years. Triumphantly standing atop the podium together would be massive, because it would be a sign that the preparations for the next Olympics were well on track.

But it wasn't just the previous two days' worth of work that was on display. This moment was a long time in the making, and the two sides had been preparing for it alongside one another every step of the way. They'd already achieved a tournament 'blackout' by both sides winning at the Cape Town Sevens a month earlier, but to do it on home soil would mean everything. In fact, according to Black Ferns Sevens star Ruby Tui, it meant more. 'The haka is an ultimate honour.

Opposite top Skipper Sarah Hirini leads the haka. MICHAEL BRADLEY/AFP VIA GETTY IMAGES

Opposite below Ruby Tui in the centre of the action during the women's final. BRETT PHIBBS/PHOTOSPORT

I don't think I feel more Kiwi than when I do that haka, it's unreal,' she said.

Her side had made it through to the final against Canada after some typically dominant form. The women's Sevens programme in New Zealand has been by far the most successful one launched in the professional era, with the team racking up 223 wins in 38 World Series tournaments since 2012; and along with that, an Olympic silver medal at Rio in 2016. They'd firmly ensconced themselves into the position a team in a black jersey should be in the eyes of the New Zealand public: it was expected that they would win, win big, and win all the time.

For the men, well that's a different story. Fans with long memories recall a time when the New Zealand Sevens side would run out with a number of actual All Blacks in it, including some of the biggest names in the game. Gone are the days of Jonah Lomu and Christian Cullen lighting up the field, and the team being a lock as World Series champions every year, though. Ironically, ever since the team was officially rebranded the All Blacks Sevens, the number of big names associated with the team has fallen steadily to the point where only Sonny Bill Williams forewent his Super Rugby commitments to chase a dream of Olympic gold. While that says an awful lot more about the pretty unrealistic expectations put on players by the 15-a-side set-up, the fact remains that for most of the past decade the All Blacks Sevens slipped a bit out of the public consciousness and definitely weren't helped when their undermanned line-up got dumped out of the Rio Olympics without a medal.

Things began to pick up once New Zealand Rugby did something they'd never done before. Clark Laidlaw, from Jedburgh, Scotland, became the first-ever foreign coach of a national rugby side. The former Scottish Sevens international took the reins after the Olympics and set about rebuilding the mana of the men's programme.

'As a Scotsman I didn't know too much about the haka,' Laidlaw admitted, 'but obviously I watched it on TV. Over the last couple of years, we've done a lot of work to understand it better, not just me but the whole team, to know what it means to us.' That work included spending time on a marae in Rotorua.

> It was important to be spending that time, eating together, sleeping in the same room and talking about why we love the team and love each other. We were trying to connect with it, learning who we're doing it for and why we're doing it. It's been quite a cool experience for me as a non-Kiwi, but also the Māori boys like Ngarohi McGarvey-Black, Regan Ware, Joe Webber who are really passionate about their roots. They've really thrived having been given the opportunity to lead this discussion. It's something we're proud of—the connection has really brought us together as a team.

It's that connection that was bringing the team success during the Hamilton tournament. From the kick-off in their first game against Wales, the All Blacks Sevens clicked perfectly. After only four minutes, they were up 21–0 and their opponents

> While the two sides had completed their historic double act together on home soil in 2020, it had been a fair few years in the making. The World Series had been held in New Zealand for 21 years up until that point, only moving to Hamilton in 2017. During the time it was in Wellington, the then men's-only tournament was dominated by the traditional superpowers of the abbreviated game, with Fiji winning three titles and England two. The All Blacks Sevens definitely benefited from the home-ground advantage, winning eight.

hadn't even touched the ball. By the time the semi-finals of the 2020 Hamilton tournament rolled around, Laidlaw was all smiles. Over the past 24 hours, they'd whipped Wales and Scotland, and comfortably beaten a strong USA side. They'd been helped by a dip in form from Fiji that'd seen the perennial powerhouse knocked out already, so all that stood in their way was Australia, then France in the final.

'Every time we select the team right now it feels like it's the biggest one,' said Laidlaw. 'There's pressure points coming, so if we can stay connected as a group we can ride through those good and bad times.'

Meanwhile, the women got off to a bit of a rusty start but clicked into gear with wins over China, England and Fiji. Michaela Blyde and Stacey Fluhler were having a race as to who could score the most tries, with both resembling characters in a video game who have unfairly programmed super-abilities. With the side since its inception in 2012, Ruby Tui can remember how they had to play in second-hand men's jerseys in their first tournament:

It just meant so much, because there's been a few of us who have been with the team ever since the re-initiation of the women's programme [in 2012]. The moment I put on my first New Zealand jersey, it was boys' size 12–14 years. I remember thinking, *Nah, that's not good enough and I'm going to be part of that change.*

That sort of attitude has, by now, made the Black Ferns Sevens the most successful team in the country. So, when both they and the men's side get through their semi-finals, it seems like it's just a matter of time before the Hamilton faithful will be able to watch them perform the haka after they've won their last match. The women had drawn Canada, the men France. At the sort of speed and skill level they were both hitting, it was difficult to see how there wasn't going to be a double blackout on the victory podium.

The Black Ferns got under way first, with the costumed and merry crowd now living and dying on every pass, kick and tackle. There was a shock, though. Despite the overwhelming favouritism, the Canadians were first to cross after some rugged play close to the line. They looked set to take a shock 7–0 lead into half-time, but a series of patient rucks and good passes put Blyde in a gap to score under the posts.

Even though the scores were level at the break, some unsurprisingly honest words were spoken among the team about the occasion and its importance. The second half saw the Black Ferns get back to doing what they do best, as Blyde streaked away again to score under the posts. The crowd roared with approval as Niall Williams showed her strength in barging over to extend the lead. Then, finally, Fluhler capped off a dominant second half with yet another try to seal the win and the trophy—precisely what the 20,000 in the stands wanted to see.

As soon as the women had left the field, the All Blacks Sevens and their French counterparts streamed on past their national flags and into the now very pleasant evening coolness. 'Same again please' was the general consensus of everyone in attendance, and they were not to be disappointed as Scott Curry charged his way over in the first possession of the game. The French hit back with a try, but then Regan Ware finished off a stunning run to give the All Blacks Sevens the lead. Curry then bagged two more in the second half to complete a very similar performance to the women: comprehensive and proud.

The pride was to be on display as the Black Ferns Sevens made their way back on to the pitch to celebrate with their brothers. The big crowd stayed on, because they'd been hoping for this moment for the whole weekend.

Black Ferns captain Sarah Hirini walked forward, amid a fair degree of nerves. She'd been out with injury for the last two tournaments, so was worried that she was a little rusty on 'Ngā Rongo Toa', the haka specifically composed for the Black Ferns Sevens.

> For me, it was the first time in a while I'd performed it. It's a special haka, made for our team, and you don't want to muck it up, especially when it's on TV! I was just trying to make sure I knew exactly what I was supposed to be doing. When we won and everything takes over, you just do it as hard as you can. Whenever we get to go out and play alongside the boys it's always about us both winning and both being successful. To do it in Hamilton was really important for both of our teams. Both teams obviously have our own processes, but we're supporting them 100 per cent and I know they're doing the same for us. To do the double was exhilarating and to run out for that final was a career highlight. The atmosphere and intensity of the crowd, it blew us away with the amount of support. We always feel it.

Hirini would know. Like Tui, she's been there from the start of the modern women's Sevens programme, through the 2016 Olympics, and now is one of the most recognisable faces in women's sport. She received a New Zealand Order of Merit in 2019 for her contribution to the sport and obvious value as a role model.

Once the Sevens sisters finished, there was an echo in the crowd. Tui, Hirini and the rest of the team looked up to see the Brazilian women's team in the stands performing 'Ka Mate'. The Brazilians, who had fought hard but lost all their games in the tournament, had been in New Zealand for over a month preparing and gaining an invaluable learning experience. The haka was to say thank you to Aotearoa.

Then the men stepped forward and ripped into 'Tū: Te Toa o Te Riri'. The Black Ferns Sevens stood staunchly behind them as Ngarohi McGarvey-Black led the haka with mere in hand. This was a special one for the men, as it was restoring a bit of mana with their first title on home soil in four years. For the past three, they'd watched from the stands as Fiji lifted the cup, having been knocked out in the semi-finals.

Laidlaw looked on, knowing full well what the moment meant to his men and their female counterparts:

> With actual friends and family in the stadium and children on the field, to watch the two teams celebrate together was really unique. There's not too many teams in the world that will ever get to do that. We've got to cherish those moments. We certainly cherished it.

Dylan Collier scores to seal a memorable tournament win for the All Blacks Sevens. HAGEN HOPKINS/ GETTY IMAGES

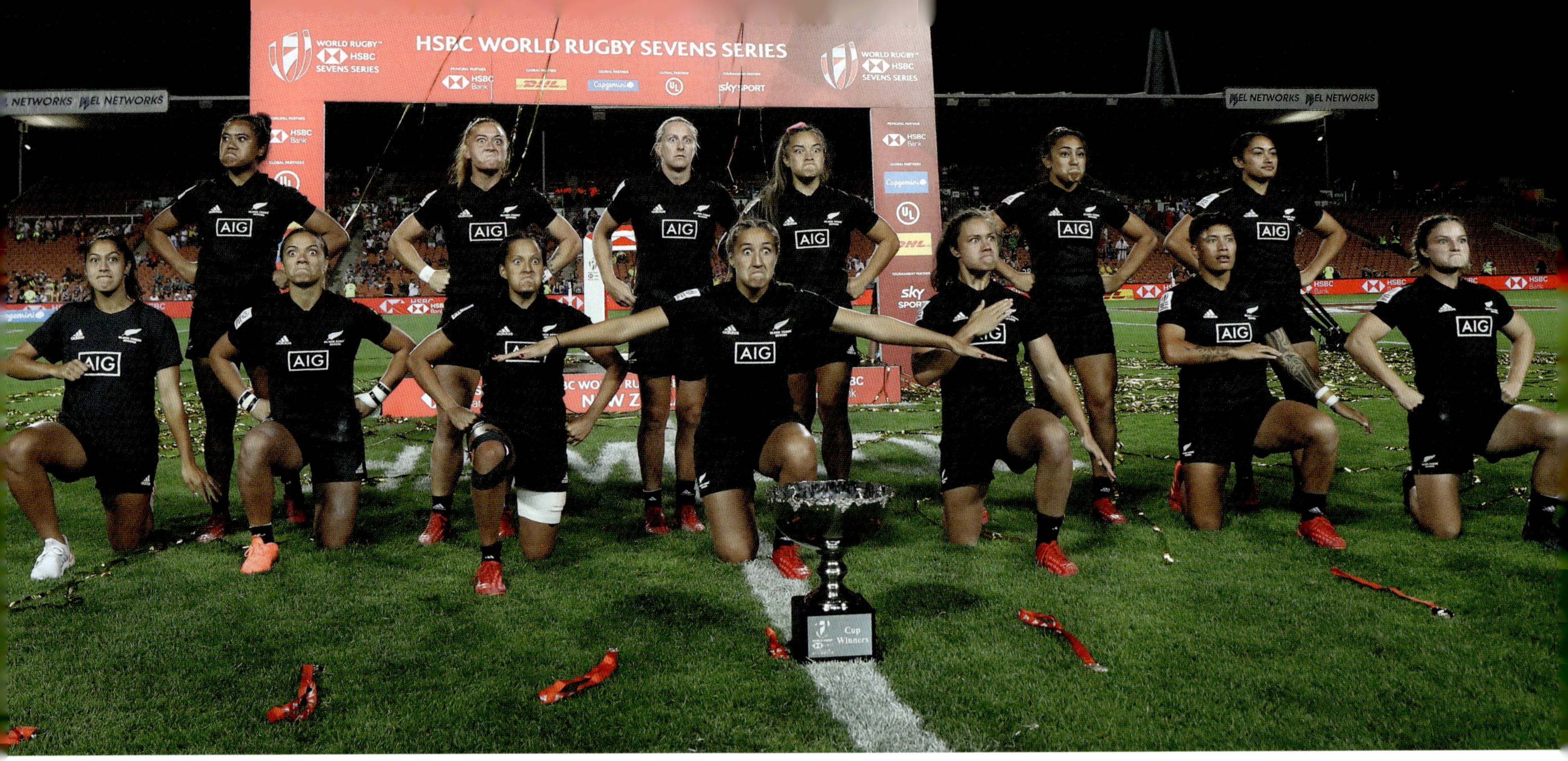
HSBC WORLD RUGBY SEVENS SERIES
WORLD RUGBY
HSBC
SEVENS SERIES
AIG
Cup Winners

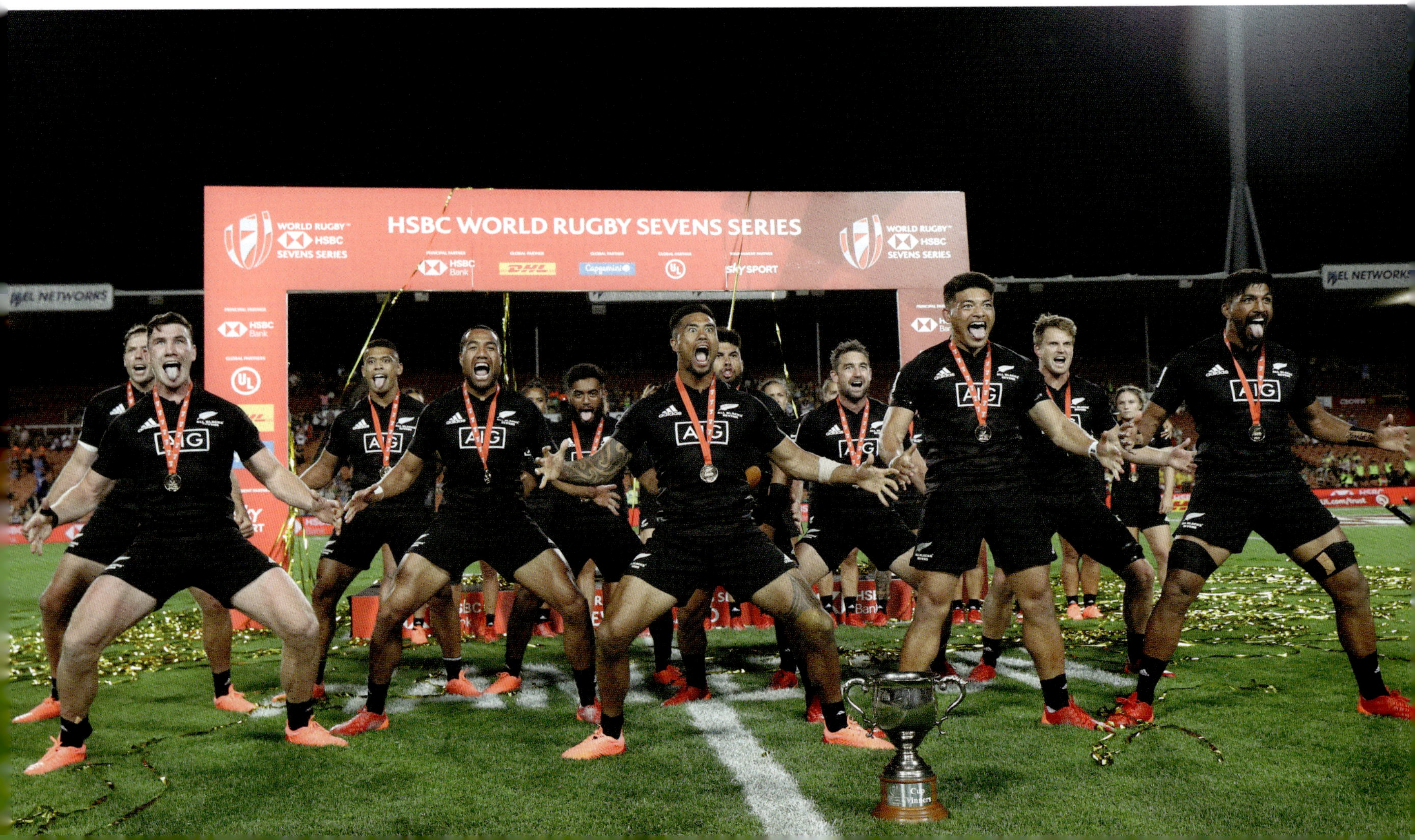
HSBC WORLD RUGBY SEVENS SERIES
WORLD RUGBY
HSBC
SEVENS SERIES
AIG

Opposite top The Black Ferns Sevens do their haka for the crowd. MICHAEL BRADLEY/AFP VIA GETTY IMAGES

Opposite below The All Blacks Sevens celebrate their tournament win in front of the fans. MICHAEL BRADLEY/AFP VIA GETTY IMAGES

Afterwards, under the grandstand, the team performed the haka again for assistant coach and former All Blacks Sevens player Tomasi Cama, who had coached his fiftieth tournament. 'In a way that's more special because it's away from everybody and about recognising his special achievement,' said Laidlaw.

Ruby Tui was adamant about how important the moment was for both sides:

> The men and women being together has been a process, it's grown. We used to be separate, but we train together and play together every day now. There's so much equality there, so when we get to do our haka and they get to do theirs, we can tautoko [support] that. It's a celebration for the whole country.

For her, it was the culmination of a great deal of thought and preparation. It'd been two long days playing gut-busting Sevens in the sun, but Tui had been visualising this moment for a lot longer.

> I practise so hard. Every time I do it I ask the whaea [senior females] in our team: 'Like this? Like that?' with my eyes and my mouth. I know if I do what I'm aiming to do tactically and technically on the rugby field, then I'll get the honour and the privilege to do the haka. When you win you can relax a little bit, but I don't think I've ever got as emotional as I did there. To be standing there in that moment with my jersey on, with my medal on, was unreal. I'd been practising the pūkana [intimidating facial expression] for that moment for honestly eight years. It went eerily silent and you could just hear us around the stadium doing our haka. I'm half-Sāmoan. The power the Māori culture has within sports is epic. It brings together not just Pākehā and Māori, but more than that because that's the category I sit in. Whenever anyone asks me about New Zealand culture, it's always the haka or war dance. Whenever we do the anthem and sing the Māori part, I remember that it was at a rugby game that it was [first] done, 20 years ago. It's so important for such a deeper reason than sport.

Her captain Hirini said that it was high time both teams should get to perform the haka not just one after another, but together:

> It was extremely special. For us to both do it at the same time because we'd won means everything. We've talked about how special it would be if we had a special Sevens haka for both teams to perform at the same time. How special would it be that a men's and women's team does a haka together?

The two sides occupy a unique spot in New Zealand rugby, indeed society, where men and women stand side by side. They are one whānau that wins and celebrates together. That night in Hamilton, said Tui, meant 'more than everything'. For her, the haka gives her strength.

'I can feel my heart pumping with blood that's a bit thicker.'

'KAPA O PANGO'

Opposite All Blacks captain Tana Umaga leads the haka in 2005. PHIL WALTER/ GETTY IMAGES

27 August 2005
Carisbrook, Dunedin

All Blacks 31
(Joe Rokocoko 2, Keven Mealamu, Leon MacDonald tries; MacDonald 3 con, pen, Luke McAlister con)

Springboks 27
(Jaque Fourie, Bryan Habana, Ricky Januarie tries; Percy Montgomery 3 con, 2 pen)

All Blacks		**Springboks**	
15	Mils Muliaina	15	Percy Montgomery
14	Rico Gear	14	Jean de Villiers
13	Tana Umaga (c)	13	Jaque Fourie
12	Aaron Mauger	12	De Wet Barry
11	Joe Rokocoko	11	Bryan Habana
10	Leon MacDonald	10	Andre Pretorius
9	Piri Weepu	9	Ricky Januarie
8	Rodney So'oialo	8	Joe van Niekerk
7	Richie McCaw	7	Juan Smith
6	Jerry Collins	6	Schalk Burger
5	Ali Williams	5	Victor Matfield
4	Chris Jack	4	Bakkies Botha
3	Carl Hayman	3	CJ van der Linde
2	Keven Mealamu	2	John Smit (c)
1	Tony Woodcock	1	Os du Randt

Reserves | | **Reserves** | |
16	Derren Whitcombe	16	Hanyani Shimange
17	Greg Somerville	17	Eddie Andrews
18	James Ryan	18	Albert van den Berg
19	Sione Lauaki	19	Jacques Cronje
20	Kevin Senio	20	Fourie du Preez
21	Luke McAlister	21	Jaco van der Westhuyzen
22	Doug Howlett	22	Marius Joubert

The Springboks form a circle to sing their national anthem. DEAN TREML/AFP VIA GETTY IMAGES

> 'We are not taking away the old haka "Ka Mate". We are adding to it, we are giving it a mate—someone to sit alongside.'
> —TANA UMAGA, ALL BLACKS CAPTAIN

THIS WAS AN ALL BLACKS haka, but one unlike anybody had seen before.

Taringa whakarongo!

Captain Tana Umaga's voice pierced the cold Dunedin night as 29,500 spectators sat transfixed.

Kia rite! Kia rite! Kia mau!
Hī!

The All Blacks crouched as one with their arms braced across their chests.

Kia whakawhenua au i ahau!
Hī, auē! Hī!

Each man dropped to one knee and pressed a fist to the turf, staring intently across at the team's old foe South Africa.

Ko Aotearoa, e ngunguru nei!
Hī, au! Au! Auē, hā! Hī!

Tana Umaga stood amid his crouching warriors, summoning all their collective energy.

Ko Kapa ŌPango, e ngunguru nei!
Hī, au! Au! Auē, hā! Hī!

The ground shuddered as the team slapped their arms in unison.

I ahahā!

Umaga slapped the back of wing Rico Gear and the team rose as one.

Ka tū te ihi-ihi
Ka tū te wanawana
Ki runga i te rangi, e tū iho nei, tū iho nei, hī!

The thumping of hands on chests echoed around the ground as the All Blacks looked to the heavens.

Ponga rā!
Kapa ŌPango! Auē, hī!
Ponga rā!
Kapa ŌPango! Auē, hī!

The All Blacks advanced towards their opponents like an unstoppable ball of energy, releasing a united roar.

Hā!

A new era for the haka had dawned.
This was 'Kapa O Pango'.

Opposite top Tana Umaga was a popular leader of the haka. PHIL WALTER/GETTY IMAGES

Opposite below Richie McCaw is airborne during the game against the Springboks. DEAN TREML/AFP VIA GETTY IMAGES

'KAPA O PANGO', WHICH translates simply to 'team in black', was written for the All Blacks by Derek Lardelli, an expert in tikanga Māori (Māori culture and customs) of the Ngāti Porou iwi. Its words and actions celebrate the land of New Zealand, the silver fern and its warriors in black.

'We are not taking away the old haka "Ka Mate". We are adding to it, we are giving it a mate—someone to sit alongside,' Tana Umaga explained to allblacks.com in 2005.

> We talked about our haka and what it meant to us. We got some leading authorities in Māori culture to come in and talk to us. We talked over a lot of aspects of the haka, about what it means to some of the new players and its effectiveness. We all left there with a greater insight into the haka and how it brought us all together—all the different cultures we have within the All Blacks.

Senior All Black Aaron Mauger was another pivotal player in the creation of 'Kapa O Pango'. 'I think the important thing about the new haka is that it talks about us and our time as All Blacks,' he said.

> You don't get a lot of time in the jersey, so you have to cherish every moment that you have. It's about doing the best that you can do when you pull the jersey on. It's about the traditions of All Blacks rugby—the black jersey, the silver fern. It's also stuff we have researched with Toi Māori and Derek Lardelli who gave us a full understanding of who we are and what it means to us.

For composer Lardelli, it was crucial that 'Kapa O Pango' told a personal story for the players who were going to perform it:

> [They] wanted a haka that said who they were, where they are from, and to create a legacy they wanted to leave for future All Blacks. 'Kapo O Pango' is about a group of young men that wanted to express themselves during haka and my job was to compose actions to that particular expression. It's about them. It talks about 'this is my time in the black jersey', 'this is my time to express myself as a player on behalf of my country'. And because they've done 'Ka Mate' so well, it was an obvious progression for them to move into creating something that would be part of their legacy.

Despite concerns around a throat-slitting gesture which would ultimately be pared back from the performance, 'Kapa O Pango' was met mostly with acclaim, but also concern from some fans who worried that its arrival would herald the end of the All Blacks' traditional 'Ka Mate' haka.

'"Ka Mate" is the foundation haka that the All Blacks have always used. "Kapa O Pango" is part of another dimension that we wish to add to and help "Kapa O Pango" and "Ka Mate" to come together,' Lardelli told allblacks.com. '"Ka Mate" is the older brother and "Kapa O Pango" is the younger brother—we are building a family of haka here.'

Greg Somerville and South Africa's Os du Randt shake hands after the match.
TOUCHLINE PHOTO/GETTY IMAGES

While there is no shortage of significance and meaning behind the creation of 'Kapa O Pango', neither was there in the choice of opponent to face the first performance of the All Blacks' new haka. It could have been easy for the All Blacks to debut 'Kapa O Pango' during the 2005 British & Irish Lions series. It was the first time the Lions had played the All Blacks in 12 years and the media contingent following the tour was like nothing New Zealand had seen before. But doing the easy thing has never been part of the All Blacks mantra.

This wasn't about grabbing global headlines or pandering to the economically rich Home Nations. This was about personal meaning and creating a legacy. South Africa, the All Blacks' greatest rival, were the only option to face 'Kapa O Pango' for the first time, on 27 August 2005. 'To stand there and watch it for the first time was a privilege,' Springboks captain John Smit said following the match. From the fans at Carisbrook that night to those watching at rugby clubs, bars or lounges around the world, the memory of Tana Umaga leading the first performance of 'Kapa O Pango' continues to send chills down the spine.

As notable as the new haka was, the match also did its part to add another chapter to the rich history of the All Blacks versus South Africa rivalry. There was plenty riding on the high-stakes encounter in chilly Dunedin. The Springboks needed a win or a draw to lift their first Tri Nations crown in 10 years, while the All Blacks required a win to keep their own title hopes alive.

The game lived up to its pre-match billing. After a seesaw encounter in which the lead swapped hands seven times, All Blacks hooker Keven Mealamu crashed over for a try with just four minutes remaining to secure the dramatic 31–27 victory. South Africa were vanquished in the deep south but showed once again why they were the All Blacks' fiercest foe.

Greater than the result, a legacy was established by the men in black that night. After more than 100 years of attachment to 'Ka Mate', the players now had their very own contemporary haka to pass down to the next generation of All Blacks. It spoke to them: who they are, where they are from, and what it means to wear the All Blacks jersey. 'Kapa O Pango' was not created to replace 'Ka Mate'. It was created to build the All Blacks' family of haka and give the players a voice.

'Ka Mate'—the older brother. 'Kapa O Pango'—the younger brother. Both sacred. Both special.

'Kapa O Pango'

Taringa whakarongo!
Kia rite! Kia rite! Kia mau!
Hī!

Kia whakawhenua au i ahau!
Hī, auē! Hī!

Ko Aotearoa, e ngunguru nei!
Hī, au! Au! Auē, hā! Hī!

Ko Kapa ŌPango, e ngunguru nei!
Hī, au! Au! Auē, hā! Hī!

I ahahā!

Ka tū te ihi-ihi

Ka tū te wanawana

Ki runga i te rangi, e tū iho nei, tū iho nei, hī!
Ponga rā!

Kapa ŌPango! Auē, hī!
Ponga rā!

Kapa ŌPango! Auē, hī!
Hā!

Let me go back to my first gasp of breath

Let my life force return to the earth

It is New Zealand that thunders now

And it is my time!
It is my moment!
The passion ignites!

This defines us as the All Blacks

And it is my time!
It is my moment!
The anticipation explodes!

Feel the power
Our dominance rises

Our supremacy emerges

To be placed on high

Silver fern!
All Blacks!
Silver fern!
All Blacks!

Auē, hī!

AN EPIC ENCOUNTER

Opposite Richard Cockerill confronts Norm Hewitt. STU FORSTER/ALLSPORT/GETTY IMAGES/HULTON ARCHIVE

22 November 1997
Old Trafford, Manchester

All Blacks 25
(Ian Jones, Taine Randell, Jeff Wilson tries; Andrew Mehrtens 2 con, 2 pen)

England 8
(Phil de Glanville try; Mike Catt pen)

All Blacks		**England**	
15	Christian Cullen	15	Matt Perry
14	Jeff Wilson	14	David Rees
13	Frank Bunce	13	Will Greenwood
12	Alama Ieremia	12	Phil de Glanville
11	Jonah Lomu	11	Adedayo Adebayo
10	Andrew Mehrtens	10	Mike Catt
9	Justin Marshall (c)	9	Kyran Bracken
8	Zinzan Brooke	8	Tony Diprose
7	Josh Kronfeld	7	Richard Hill
6	Taine Randell	6	Lawrence Dallaglio (c)
5	Robin Brooke	5	Garath Archer
4	Ian Jones	4	Martin Johnson
3	Olo Brown	3	Darren Garforth
2	Norm Hewitt	2	Richard Cockerill
1	Craig Dowd	1	Jason Leonard

Reserves

16	Andrew Blowers	16	Neil Back
17	Scott McLeod	17	Austin Healey
18	Jon Preston	18	Paul Grayson
19	Mark Allen	19	Graham Rowntree
20	Anton Oliver	20	Andy Long
21	Charles Riechelmann	21	Danny Grewcock

Martin Johnson and referee Peter Marshall flank the showdown between Norm Hewitt and Richard Cockerill. JOHN GILES/PA IMAGES VIA GETTY IMAGES

'It's a challenge, they want to smash you, you want to smash them, alright you want to take this on, let's have a crack.'
—RICHARD COCKERILL, ENGLAND HOOKER

THE FIRST TEST BETWEEN the All Blacks and England in the professional age is remembered most not for the action on the pitch, but instead for an epic encounter between hookers Norm Hewitt and Richard Cockerill during the haka.

Before kick-off there was a huge sense of expectation hanging in the ice-cold air at Old Trafford. Not only was the match being played at the home of the legendary Manchester United football club, but also it was the first test between the sides since Jonah Lomu had terrorised England in a four-try assault at the 1995 Rugby World Cup.

The build-up to the test had captivated both England and New Zealand with images of the All Blacks training on the hallowed Old Trafford pitch and meeting with Manchester United manager Sir Alex Ferguson being beamed around the world.

England had not played in Manchester for more than half a century and were desperate to make their mark on one of the world's most famous sporting arenas. Two young hookers were also keen to make an impact on the game. For All Blacks hooker Norm Hewitt it was a rare start, with regular hooker and captain Sean Fitzpatrick out through injury. On the other side of the park, it was a first test start for England's Richard Cockerill and a chance to make the number 2 jersey his own.

With Hewitt to lead the haka for the All Blacks, and Cockerill widely noted for his fiery temperament, the collision course was set in front of a capacity Old Trafford crowd. As told to Sky Sports UK, Cockerill picks up the story following the anthems: 'It was my first start in a test match and I was obviously quite excitable. I just thought, *I'm going to find Norm and stand opposite him and say, "C'mon mate let's have a go".*' What followed was one of the most intense personal confrontations ever witnessed during an All Blacks haka.

As Norm Hewitt prepared to lead the haka, Cockerill advanced over the halfway line towards his opposite. 'It's a challenge, they want to smash you, you want to smash them, alright you want to take this on, let's have a crack,' Cockerill said. Those at the ground could feel the adrenalin surge as Hewitt launched into a rousing haka and Cockerill responded with an indecipherable verbal spray.

With the hulking men standing eyeball to eyeball, referee Peter Marshall attempted to intervene but quickly retreated for fear of being caught in the crossfire. A shove from Cockerill barely broke Hewitt's stride as he finished the haka and stared down his challenger. After one last verbal barb, Cockerill turned back in search of support from his team. 'Johnno [Martin Johnson]

Below Kiwi support for the All Blacks. ROSS SETFORD/GETTY IMAGES

Opposite top Norm Hewitt leaves the field after the draw with England at Twickenham in December 1997. ANDREW CORNAGA/PHOTOSPORT

Opposite below Jonah Lomu has words with Cockerill during a test match at Eden Park. ROSS LAND/GETTY IMAGES

was standing quite close to me and we turned around for the kick-off and I looked at him hoping for a bit of advice and he said, "What the f**k have you done?"'

Although the challenge almost boiled over to a physical confrontation in the middle of Old Trafford, Hewitt is quick to dismiss any notion of disrespect from the England team. In his 2001 biography, *Gladiator: The Norm Hewitt Story* by Michael Laws, Hewitt said:

> I didn't think he or the English players were disrespecting the haka. People who say that miss the point of what the haka is about. It's a challenge—a challenge to war. And the Poms had exactly the right answer to it—you accept the challenge and you throw it back. But, I'll tell you this—I was one motivated Māori boy that afternoon! And I made sure Cockerill knew it too.

As it turned out, Cockerill's up-close and personal confrontation with Hewitt would be as near as England would come to getting the better of the All Blacks that day. The men in black didn't quite run rampant but they were never really tested, and they crossed for three tries to secure a comfortable 25–8 victory.

The eyebrow-raising moments weren't done with once the final whistle was blown, though. Lawrence Dallaglio's side famously performed a lap of honour to show their gratitude to the normally football-mad crowd at Old Trafford. It was an interesting act to bookmark what was a frustrating effort from England in a highly hyped test match.

Despite the result not going in England's favour, Cockerill said he wouldn't change anything about the way he faced the haka for the first time. 'I believe that I did the right thing that day,' he said. 'They were throwing down a challenge and I showed them I was ready to accept it. I'm sure they would rather we did that than walk away.'

Just two weeks later, England showed why they are one of the All Blacks' greatest rivals by drawing 26–26 at their home fortress of Twickenham. Hewitt and Cockerill started in the number 2 jersey once again but avoided any pre-match theatrics in what turned out to be a truly classic test match.

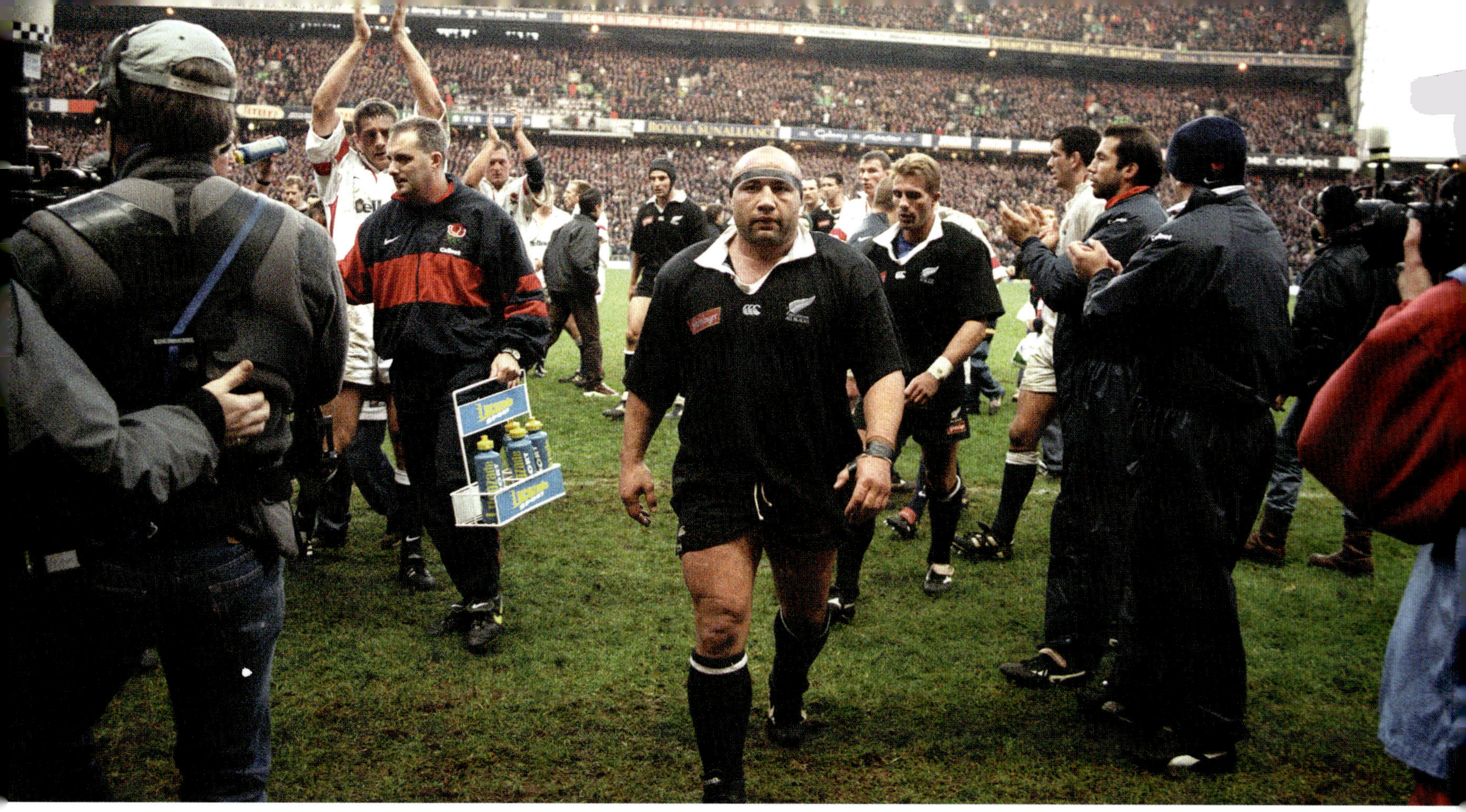
ROYAL & SUN ALLIANCE

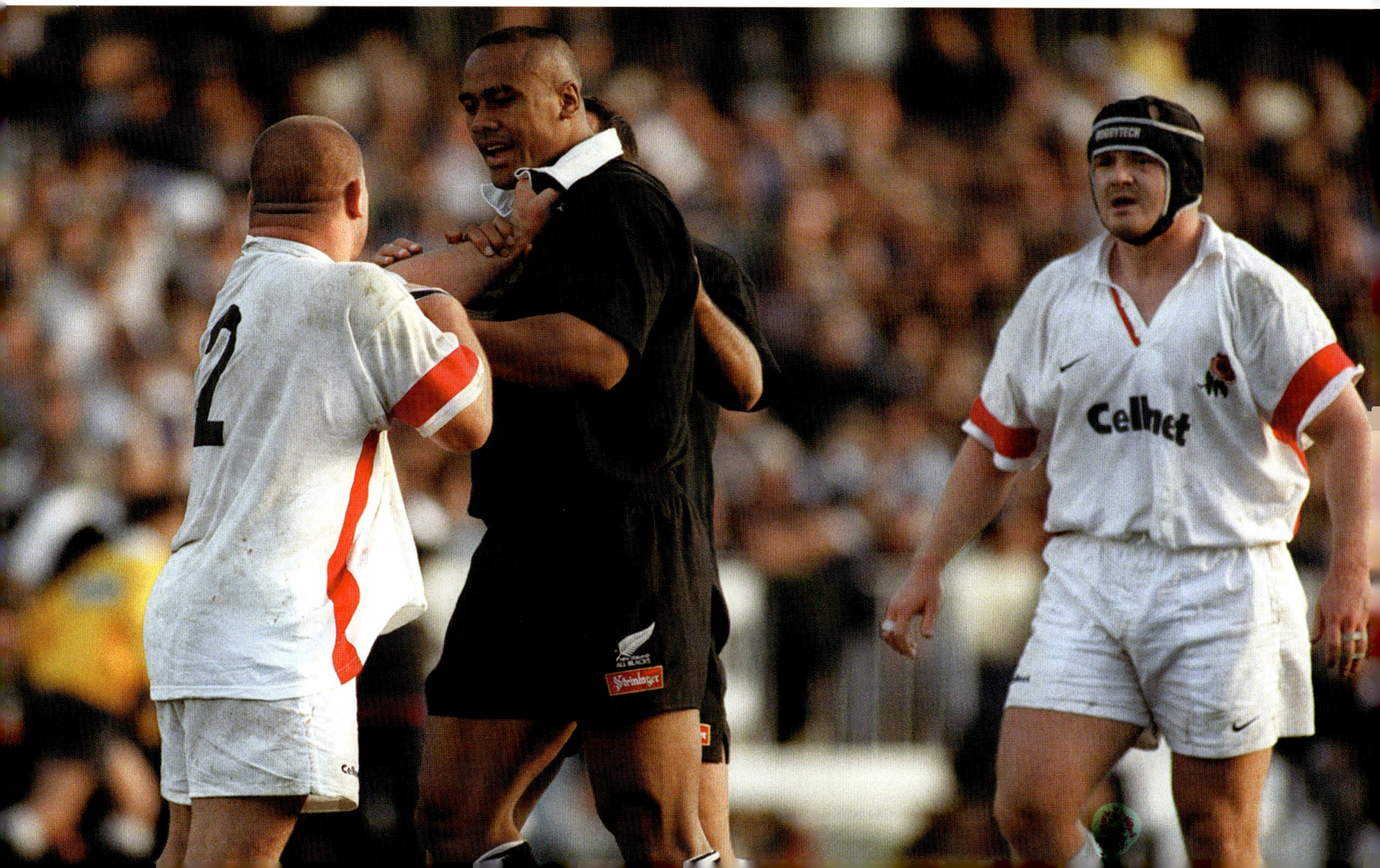
Cellnet
Steinlager

THE HAKA'S HOLLYWOOD CONNECTION

Opposite Jason Momoa and his treasured All Blacks jersey. DEVIN MANKY/ICON SPORTSWIRE VIA GETTY IMAGES

20 October 1991
Stade Nord, Lille

All Blacks 29
(John Timu 2, Zinzan Brooke, John Kirwan, Bernie McCahill tries; Grant Fox 3 con, pen)

Canada 13
(Al Charron, Chris Tynan tries; Mark Wyatt pen, Gareth Rees con)

All Blacks	Canada
15 John Timu	15 Mark Wyatt (c)
14 John Kirwan	14 Scott Stewart
13 Craig Innes	13 Christian Stewart
12 Bernie McCahill	12 Tom Woods
11 Va'aiga Tuigamala	11 Steve Gray
10 Grant Fox	10 Gareth Rees
9 Graeme Bachop	9 Chris Tynan
8 Zinzan Brooke	8 Glenn Ennis
7 Paul Henderson	7 Gord MacKinnon
6 Alan Whetton	6 Al Charron
5 Gary Whetton (c)	5 Norm Hadley
4 Ian Jones	4 Ron van den Brink
3 Richard Loe	3 Paul Szabo
2 Sean Fitzpatrick	2 David Speirs
1 Steve McDowall	1 Eddie Evans

Reserves	Reserves
16 Jon Preston	16 Pat Palmer
17 Walter Little	17 John Lecky
18 Jason Hewett	18 John Graf
19 Andy Earl	19 Roy Radu
20 Mark Carter	20 Gary Dukelow
21 Graham Dowd	21 Karl Svoboda

The All Blacks do the haka before their match with Canada. JEROME PREVOST/TEMPSPORT/CORBIS/VCG VIA GETTY IMAGES

> 'So, there I was, facing the haka and trying not to look fazed by it. I was thinking, I'm about to play my rugby heroes, guys that I've only seen in magazines or on video and here they are standing opposite me doing the haka.'
>
> —AL CHARRON, MAPLE LEAFS NUMBER 6

CANADA'S VERY FIRST TEST clash against the All Blacks at the 1991 Rugby World Cup still stands out as their most competitive and memorable encounter against New Zealand.

The Maple Leafs were impressive in pool play with wins over Romania (19–11) and Fiji (13–3) and a close loss to France (19–13) to set up a quarter-final showdown with the All Blacks. The All Blacks were the inaugural holders of the Webb Ellis Cup and yet to taste defeat in tournament play with wins over England, USA and Italy following on from their unbeaten run at the 1987 tournament.

The Gary Whetton-led side may not have been as dominant in pool stages as they were in 1987 but were still expected to walk over an unheralded Canadian team in Lille. Talismanic Canadian loose forward Al Charron explained that for many of his team, it was a dream come true to simply play against the All Blacks:

> Finding any footage of the All Blacks was hard when I started playing rugby in the 1980s. You had to rely on tapes being passed around or magazine clippings. There were players in my club who got their hands on tapes and said if you want to get better you have to watch the All Blacks. I started watching it and the haka was all new to me. Lo and behold, a few years later I found myself playing against the All Blacks at the Rugby World Cup.

With the rain pelting down in Lille, Charron said it was a surreal moment facing the All Blacks haka.

> I was off to the side of the haka to begin with. I don't know what happened but next thing I shifted over and was more in the middle. So, there I was, facing the haka and trying not to look fazed by it. I was thinking, *I'm about to play my rugby heroes, guys that I've only seen in magazines or on video and here they are standing opposite me doing the haka.*

Despite trying to not look intimidated, Charron said that the haka had served to 'pump up' and galvanise the Canadian team before the biggest game of their lives.

> We were quite proud of that game. We knew we were playing a better side but tried to match them physically. In the first half they took some opportunistic tries and took the game to us. In the second half we outscored them 10–8. They beat us by 16 points in the

Opposite top Stoked, bro—Momoa celebrates as the All Blacks Sevens score. DEVIN MANKY/ICON SPORTSWIRE VIA GETTY IMAGES

Opposite below Zinzan Brooke in action, wearing the jersey that found its way to Momoa years later. SIMON BRUTY/ALLSPORT

end, but it was a terrific performance from Canada to push the reigning champions close.

The 29–13 loss remains Canada's best effort against the All Blacks in six attempts (as of 2019) and marks the only time Canada have kept the All Blacks below 50 points. It also stands as Canada's only knockout appearance at a Rugby World Cup and the high point of a golden era for Canadian rugby where first five-eighth Gareth Rees and centre Christian Stewart were considered among the world's best players.

MANY YEARS LATER, THE All Blacks versus Canada quarter-final entered rugby folklore for another reason altogether. At the 2019 Vancouver Sevens, Hollywood actor Jason Momoa was seen sporting a match-worn All Blacks jersey from the early 1990s. Fans quickly speculated about the origin of the jersey and wondered how Momoa came into possession of such a precious taonga. After being inundated with questions on social media, the *Game of Thrones* and *Aquaman* star revealed to allblacks.com just where it had come from:

> It was a gift from my stuntman Glenn Ennis about 15 years ago when I was on *Stargate Atlantis*. He played for Canada against the All Blacks at the 1991 Rugby World Cup where he traded jerseys with the legendary Zinzan Brooke.

Former All Blacks number 8 Brooke was watching the Vancouver Sevens on TV from his home in England when he spotted Momoa wearing the retro All Blacks jersey:

> Aquaman [Momoa] was in the VIP section but was very accommodating and engaging with the fans. When he turned around, I saw that he had a number 8 jersey. I thought, *That's just pure coincidence. That looks like a real jersey.* And, lo and behold, it is. I was delighted. When Ali [Brooke's wife] told me the story, I thought, *Wow, that is very cool that it just happens to be the jersey I wore.*

'He was great on *Aquaman*,' added the 58-test loose forward. 'What was pleasing for me, though, was that he took the time out to talk to and engage with the fans. He grabbed the phones and took the photos. His feet have not left the ground.'

The Hawai'ian-born actor has since professed his love and respect for the All Blacks and even performed a haka alongside New Zealand screen icon Temuera Morrison at the premiere of his blockbuster hit *Aquaman*. Considered one of the most popular movie stars in the world, Momoa still holds a special place in his heart for Zinzan's 1991 Rugby World Cup jersey, saying, 'It is one of the greatest presents I have ever been given. I never leave home without it. It always travels with me.'

CHIP ON THE SHOULDER

Opposite British & Irish Lions captain Brian O'Driscoll accepts the challenge from the All Blacks. DAVID DAVIES/PA IMAGES VIA GETTY IMAGES

25 June 2005
Jade Stadium, Christchurch

All Blacks 21
(Sitiveni Sivivatu, Ali Williams tries; Dan Carter 3 pen, con)

Lions 3
(Jonny Wilkinson pen)

All Blacks

15 Leon MacDonald
14 Doug Howlett
13 Tana Umaga (c)
12 Aaron Mauger
11 Sitiveni Sivivatu
10 Dan Carter
9 Justin Marshall
8 Rodney So'oialo
7 Richie McCaw
6 Jerry Collins
5 Ali Williams
4 Chris Jack
3 Carl Hayman
2 Keven Mealamu
1 Tony Woodcock

Reserves

16 Derren Witcombe
17 Greg Somerville
18 Jono Gibbes
19 Sione Lauaki
20 Byron Kelleher
21 Mils Muliaina
22 Rico Gear

British & Irish Lions

15 Jason Robinson
14 Josh Lewsey
13 Brian O'Driscoll (c)
12 Jonny Wilkinson
11 Gareth Thomas
10 Stephen Jones
9 Dwayne Peel
8 Martin Corry
7 Neil Back
6 Richard Hill
5 Ben Kay
4 Paul O'Connell
3 Julian White
2 Shane Byrne
1 Gethin Jenkins

Reserves

16 Steve Thompson
17 Graham Rowntree
18 Danny Grewcock
19 Ryan Jones
20 Matt Dawson
21 Will Greenwood
22 Shane Horgan

The All Blacks lay down their challenge to the Lions. DEAN TREML/GETTY IMAGES

'We spread out in a half-moon shape, with me out front as the leader and the youngest member, Dwayne Peel, standing behind me. When the haka ends, I pull up some grass and throw it at them, as if pulling the ground from underneath their feet.'

—BRIAN O'DRISCOLL,
BRITISH & IRISH LIONS CAPTAIN

THERE ARE TIMES WHEN figuring out a way to counter the haka works. Then, as in the case of the 2005 British & Irish Lions, there are times when it definitely doesn't. That tour to New Zealand has gone down as one of the biggest disasters in the illustrious composite side's history—indeed, it almost meant that the whole idea of the Lions was consigned to the pages of history books and memories.

They arrived on Aotearoa's shores to much pomp and ceremony, and left with their tails between their legs and a 3–0 series drubbing on their record. Their coach, Sir Clive Woodward, had his reputation as a World Cup-winning genius treated as if it were on the wrong side of a ruck back in the days when men wore 17-millimetre steel sprigs. Their captain, Brian O'Driscoll, lasted only a matter of seconds into the first test against the All Blacks before he left the field with an injury to (and chip on) his shoulder that forced him out of the tour.

That moment of infamy is the one that the tour is most remembered for by UK rugby fans, not least because it's become a touchpoint of instant controversy for pundits whenever the All Blacks and the Lions are mentioned in the same sentence. For All Blacks fans and many others, the second test in Wellington would arguably be Dan Carter's greatest test in a black jersey. But before the series kicked off in Christchurch—with a test that on paper promised to resemble some of the tightly fought encounters between these opponents in the past—the Lions attempted to counter the haka with a tactic that deserves a bit of recognition. In fact, it has been emulated with success in the years since.

TOURING HAS NEVER BEEN an easy task for rugby sides. Developed in the nineteenth century as a way of maximising exposure and potential profits from a series of games, back in those days it made sense to load up the schedule with as many fixtures as possible. The earliest New Zealand tour to the British Isles lasted over a year and 107 matches, so it's fair to say that they started at the top end of the scale and worked their way back down. The Lions had been coming to New Zealand in a few guises since 1888, but didn't have the legendary name and jerseys that are so familiar to us until the 1950 tour. There was one very notable success, in 1971, when a dream team of British stars managed to outplay the All Blacks at their own game and win a series 2–1. But other than that, it had been lean pickings for the men in red in the land of the long white cloud.

The 2005 tour was the first Lions visit to New

Opposite The New Zealand Māori perform a haka as the Lions watch on. DEAN TREML/GETTY IMAGES

Zealand in the professional era. This meant a squad unlike anyone had ever seen before, all under the control of Woodward, the mastermind of England's breakthrough Rugby World Cup win in Australia two years earlier: 44 players and 28 support staff, including 10 coaches, a legal adviser, a former referee and former head political communications adviser Alastair Campbell as media manager. That bloated party list immediately raised eyebrows, but the team's preparation before they even left home raised questions. Flanker Lewis Moody recalled that the team was expected to attend media training classes with Campbell two days out from their first match, a home fixture against Argentina, instead of using the precious little time available to perfect their on-field combinations. Lock Donncha O'Callaghan wasn't particularly enthusiastic about the team-building exercises either, one of which involved the rugby players painting a giant mural. The no-nonsense Irishman had more traditional views on how to bring a team together, saying: 'Let them kick the shit out of each other on the training field or let them go out on the piss for a night.'

As it turned out, the Lions probably should have spent more time on lineouts and scrums than handling reporters and honing their art skills. The test against Argentina in Cardiff ended up being a much sterner challenge than at first thought, and the Lions had to rely on the boot of Jonny Wilkinson to escape with a 25-all draw. They really should have done a bit more homework on their opposition as well, as the Pumas side contained the nucleus of the team that would finish third at the next World Cup. However, this was the Lions' first hit-out together and it's not an easy task trying to coax cohesion out of players who spend the Six Nations desperately trying to annihilate one another. The 2005 Lions nonetheless set off for New Zealand to play three tests and seven midweek games against various provincial sides. What awaited them was a nation that saw the tour as an opportunity to right some of the wrongs of the World Cup that Woodward and his Englishmen had won, and in which the All Blacks had underperformed.

To mark the first Lions tour to New Zealand of the professional era, and the first since 1993, the occasion was hyped up by the NZRU and its sponsors and advertisers. Tickets for each match were snapped up months in advance, with the public having to go into a ballot for the chance to fork out the highest prices the country had ever seen for attending a rugby game. There was expected to be an invasion of British supporters, with the hospitality industry licking its lips at the prospect of emptying the fat wallets of the visitors on a regular basis throughout the month-and-a-half long tour.

The tour actually started pretty well for the Lions, with a couple of assured wins over Bay of Plenty and Taranaki. These were the days when provincial rugby in New Zealand actually represented the decent depth in playing talent that existed, rather than the glorified age-grade tournament it is now, so those results sparked a bit of hope that the test side could actually beat the All Blacks. But before the test series began, there was to be a very serious other challenge—so much so that it was being dubbed the 'fourth test'. The Lions had to get through a very strong

New Zealand Māori side at Waikato Stadium, which contained the likes of Carl Hayman, Luke McAlister, Piri Weepu and Carlos Spencer.

Before kick-off, though, the Lions management had devised something new to showcase their pride in the team. An anthem, called 'The Power of Four', had been composed and was played after the teams lined up on the field. The only problem was that it wasn't very good, providing an embarrassing spectacle as the team stood stone-faced throughout the funeral-like dirge, refusing to sing or even look like they were enjoying it. Quickly becoming an unwanted delay to proceedings before each game, the song proved equally unpopular with the fans as well.

After that cringe-worthy exercise, the Lions' shadow test side found themselves lining up on halfway to face 'Te Tīmatanga', which the Māori side (they wouldn't officially be rebranded as the Māori All Blacks for another seven years) had been performing since 2001. It tells the story

> The Lions were greeted on their arrival to New Zealand with the sight of an advertising campaign by adidas that played on the familiar crouch of the All Blacks at the start of the haka. Called 'Haka Man', the mysterious silhouette started appearing around the country in the weeks leading up to the tour, including two 50-metre renditions on paddocks in the Canterbury plains and outside Queenstown. Seven-metre statues were put up in Dunedin's Octagon, Christchurch Square, Invercargill, Taupō and Wellington's Te Papa museum, while a 12.5-metre image was erected on State Highway 2 on the way to Rotorua. As well as the large edifices, temporary tattoos and stickers made sure that Haka Man was omnipresent throughout the tour as a counter to the traditionally gigantic Lions supporters party.

Opposite top The Lions enjoyed massive support wherever they played in New Zealand. DEAN TREML/ GETTY IMAGES

Opposite below The New Zealand Māori (renamed the Māori All Blacks in 2012) defeat the Lions. ROSS LAND/GETTY IMAGES

of creation, not only of the Earth but also of the warriors and chiefs who take the battlefield, and their quest for unity, strength and knowledge.

> *Whakakī ki te Maunga*
> *Tae ki te Whenua*
> *Hoki ki te Rangi*
> *Tae ki te Pukerunga*
>
> *If you aim for the mountains*
> *you will hit the plains*
> *if you aim for the sky*
> *you will hit the mountain peaks*

'That haka was from near where it was played in Waikato; the royalty of Māori is based near there,' remembered Māori captain and flanker Jono Gibbes. 'It's a strong, traditional area of New Zealand. It was a good opportunity to welcome them on to the field and an appropriate welcome on the area where we stood. It certainly increased the intensity.'

Led by Rua Tipoki, the Māori side had their voices amplified over the then recently rebuilt Waikato Stadium. It had been home to perhaps the most famous midweek tour game in New Zealand rugby history, when the 1956 Waikato side defeated the Springboks, but now it was about to be the scene of another epic encounter. The Māori had fashioned a formidable record over the previous decade, with only two losses in the 20 matches since they'd last played the Lions in 1993. One of those was to the then world-champion Wallabies in 2001, the other to the English side that would go on to win the World Cup in 2003. Some were even predicting that this would be a sterner challenge for the Lions than the test matches themselves.

What eventuated was a brutal, tense affair for the first half. Both sets of forwards barrelled into each other with ferocious frequency, with the Lions showing that they were more than up for the challenge laid down by the Māori pre-game. Matt Dawson gave them the first spark of an attack after 14 minutes when he burst into the Māori 22, which drew a penalty that Stephen Jones slotted to take the early lead. Deacon Manu got the better of Julian White at a scrum not long after and the Lions were penalised, which David Hill banged over to level the scores. The two sides traded another shot at goal each to make it 6-all at half-time.

By now, the June temperature had cooled down sufficiently for a haze of evaporating sweat to be rising off each player, giving the field that eerie, misty look favoured by filmmakers and photographers who want to capture the essence of the New Zealand landscape—albeit populated by 30 men smashing away at each other for all they were worth. The Māori took the lead when McAlister nudged over another penalty to make the score 9–6, and for a while there it looked like it might stay like that. But the Māori desperately wanted a try and found themselves with a lineout on the Lions' five-metre line. The ball went to Spencer, who doubled around Tipoki and then sent it wide to Leon MacDonald. There was no discernible gap for MacDonald to run through, so he cut back and headed straight into the path of three Lions defenders, carried them to a metre

Opposite top The controversial Alastair Campbell. PHIL WALTER/ GETTY IMAGES

Opposite below Lions lock Donncha O'Callaghan acknowledges the crowd following his team's win over Otago. ROSS LAND/ GETTY IMAGES

out, and then stretched his arm over the line to plant the ball.

That was it. There were still 20 minutes to go but the Māori had put enough distance between themselves and the Lions. Brian O'Driscoll scored a consolation try to make the dying minutes interesting but the clock ran out, the game ending in a famous 19–13 win for the New Zealand Māori. Quoted in *The Guardian*, Gibbes described the mood in the changing rooms as 'euphoric', but the celebrations afterwards as somewhat muted:

> We went back to our hotel, and had a couple of beers in a room to acknowledge what we'd done, but that team would never play again together. We lived together for the week, and that was it. You try and live in that moment. Some lads went into town, but I was so knackered. I had a full house of extended family at my place. They helped themselves to the fridge, and I went to bed.

Tellingly, the Lions barely mixed with their vanquishers after the game, staying for a formal dinner then leaving immediately to go back to Auckland. This was essentially the first mark in the loss column for the test side, and things weren't going to get any easier in a fortnight's time when they were due to play the All Blacks.

TO THEIR CREDIT, THE Lions did bounce back with three successive wins in their provincial matches, over Otago, Wellington and Southland. It's worth noting that by now the stronger unions had been shorn of their All Blacks, so while Wellington were in one of the strongest periods of their history, the team that was put out to face the Lions was rather undergunned and featured several players on debut. Also, by now there were problems in the touring squad, which had effectively divided itself into the test and midweek sides that were having little to do with each other. The midweekers found themselves locked out of test-team planning meetings, which did little to enhance morale. 'It was obvious to a lot of fellas that the XV for the first test was already picked—probably before we'd even left home,' said O'Callaghan.

Meanwhile, according to some players, Campbell was proving to be more of a hindrance than anything else. The press man, who at the time was in the midst of a passionate but ultimately ill-fated PR campaign for Lance Armstrong's cancer charity, attempted to portray the relationship between Woodward and Welsh star Gavin Henson as far rosier than it actually was. Fabricated quotes and out-of-context photographs that suggested all was well were distributed, when in reality Henson was livid at his non-selection for the test side.

In addition, the overthinking from the coaching staff was getting too much for the players to handle. Dawson recalled going 'into the game with the most complex set of calls I have ever known, so complex that the players didn't understand them. Two days before the first test on supposedly the best organised of all Lions tours, no one knew where the ball was going.' One thing they did

Opposite Matt Dawson walks off the field dejected following the first test against the All Blacks. PHIL WALTER/GETTY IMAGES

know, however, was how they were going to stand in front of the haka before the first test got under way at Christchurch's Jade Stadium. They'd sought some advice and come up with a unique strategy which they believed would respect the haka and challenge it at the same time.

'We spread out in a half-moon shape, with me out front as the leader and the youngest member, Dwayne Peel, standing behind me,' said O'Driscoll. 'When the haka ends, I pull up some grass and throw it at them, as if pulling the ground from underneath their feet.'

The haka that the All Blacks performed on that freezing-cold night in Christchurch was 'Ka Mate', led by Rico Gear. The watching public didn't know it at the time, but it would be one of the last occasions when the All Blacks would have only one haka available to them. The Lions spread right across the width of the field for their reply, with the outer edges of their player-formed crescent almost on the touchlines. The All Blacks responded with a powerful version of the challenge, while O'Driscoll snatched at the grass with his gloved hand and threw it back in his opposition's direction.

Matt Dawson wasn't sure that the gesture had achieved the intended effect, however. The look on his face as he left the pitch to take his seat on the reserves bench was one of worry rather than confidence. He commented later that 'the All Blacks looked at us with an expression that does not suggest gratitude at the respect we believe we have just paid to their heritage'. Two of the men staring across at O'Driscoll were Tana Umaga and Keven Mealamu. What they did next would go down in test rugby history, but not for the right reasons.

After Wilkinson had launched the ball into the air from the kick-off, the All Blacks forwards took it into a very tightly fought ruck. After being awarded a penalty, Justin Marshall caught the Lions on the hop when he tapped and went, a move which eventually saw Dan Carter run the ball up to halfway. The ball went wide out to the far sideline, where the Lions had positioned one side of their formation during the haka. As the All Blacks sped up the play, Leon MacDonald, the hero from the Māori game, took it into contact and was tackled by O'Driscoll and Gareth Thomas. The ruck slowed play down and the All Blacks captain found himself standing over the Lions captain, who had just thrown some blades of grass at him. Together with Mealamu, he picked the Irishman up and dumped him heavily on his shoulder.

A shoulder dislocation can come in a few different forms of seriousness, but there is one symptom that encompasses them all: severe pain. That's exactly what O'Driscoll found himself in on the Christchurch turf, clutching at his right shoulder as a medic ran on to attend to him. Meanwhile, Carter had sent an almost perfect kick into the corner that only just collided with the corner post instead of going into touch and set the All Blacks up with a try-scoring opportunity inside the first minute of play. After a lengthy delay, O'Driscoll was carted off the field. The story of that injury had only just begun, but it's fair to say that given the play leading up to it, it was highly

Opposite Lions captain Brian O'Driscoll is tended to by the team doctor before leaving the field with a suspected dislocated shoulder. CORBIS/SPORTSFILE VIA GETTY IMAGES

unlikely that O'Driscoll would have had any effect on the game anyway.

That's because the All Blacks kept up their assault on the Lions' line with renewed ferocity. This was, after all, a team that was still hurting from being knocked out of the World Cup two years previously by a Wallabies side that in turn lost to England in the final. That was the same England side that had come to Wellington in 2003 and beaten the All Blacks, so any complaints that they hadn't faced the true strength of world rugby in the tournament didn't carry much weight. While it's true that the All Blacks had defeated the English three times in 2004, this Lions tour was seen very much as a way to put things right, with coach Graham Henry promoting Carter to be his full-time playmaker and installing Umaga as the All Blacks' first-ever Pasifika test captain.

The home side seemed destined to breach the Lions' line after 12 minutes, when only a massively cynical play by Paul O'Connell stopped them. The Irish lock came from a mile offside to take out Chris Jack as he looked to pass from the base of a ruck only a metre out with a two-man overlap on his right. O'Connell was yellow carded, which only underlined the writing that was already on the wall. 'We are cannon fodder,' said Jonny Wilkinson. 'It's helpless. I get so frustrated and very fired up. I start looking for big hits everywhere, whether they are on or not, to try and change the game. I don't know how else we are going to achieve anything.'

By this stage the biting cold was starting to get to the Lions, this being the South Island on a winter's night, after all. Stephen Jones' brain froze when they were awarded a penalty on their own 10-metre line, and instead of kicking for touch he launched a futile cross-kick that went straight into Umaga's hands on the All Blacks' 22. Only Josh Lewsey had made an effort to get to the ball, and he was swatted aside as the All Blacks counterattacked. MacDonald surged down the wing and looked destined to score, only to be bundled into touch by Ryan Jones. The Lions thought they'd got off the hook, but the lineout call was missed and the ball from Shane Byrne went straight into Ali Williams' hands. Williams charged 20 metres to score the most important test try of his career.

The All Blacks' next try was arguably the insult added to O'Driscoll's injury. The second half had barely got under way when Aaron Mauger barrelled over Jones and put Umaga into the gap that O'Driscoll would have been covering. Twenty metres later and Umaga sent out one of the most pinpoint passes in the history of test rugby, spinning the ball across almost a third of the width of the field before it thudded perfectly onto the chest of Sitiveni Sivivatu. The winger cut in, leaving Lewsey flat on his backside and Jason Robinson clutching at thin air. The Fijian-born Sivivatu slid over the tryline, getting the freezing and mostly plastic-bag-clad crowd on their feet. An icy dagger plunged straight into the heart of an already terminal Lions team meant that the score ended 21–3 to the All Blacks, but it might as well have been a 100-point margin.

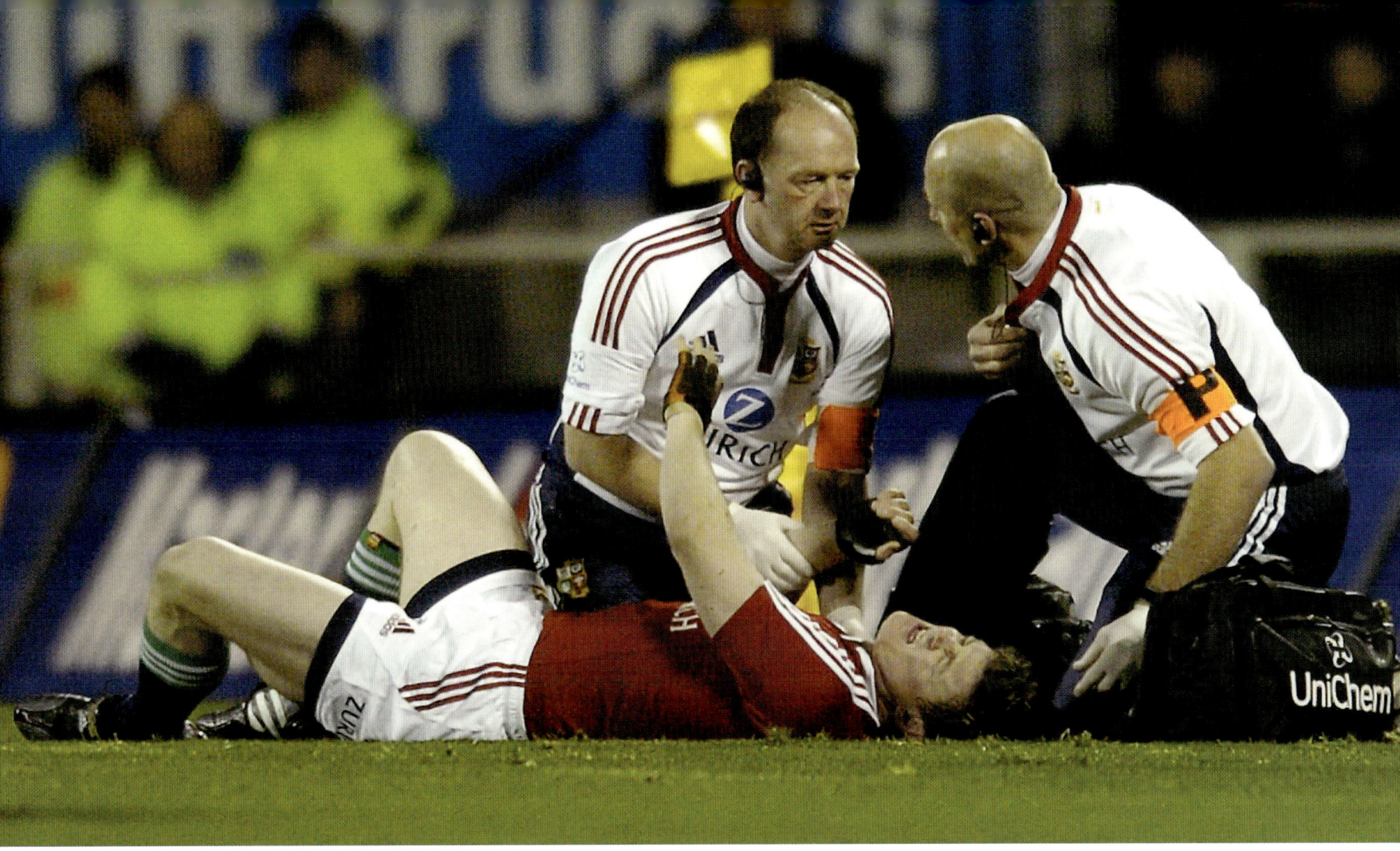

Not that the Lions' rugby shortcomings were what Woodward and Campbell wanted to talk about in the aftermath. 'From this point to the end of the trip there is no other topic of conversation than how Brian was treated and how those responsible got away with it,' said Dawson. The actions of the two senior All Blacks, Umaga and Mealamu, were spun into the greatest crime in the history of sports as the Lions management called a special press conference at midnight on the Sunday following the test. While it was an undeniably brutal way to deal with the Lions' skipper, on the scale of dirty rugby acts it didn't exactly rate as highly as, say, eye-gouging or grabbing someone's private parts. Things got worse when the match citing commissioner decided that the pair didn't have a case to answer and were free to play the following week; then worse still when Lions lock Danny Grewcock did get suspended for biting Mealamu.

The Lions roared with outrage, claiming a home-town bias that had seen the seemingly deliberate injuring of their skipper go unpunished. O'Driscoll, for his part, wasn't about to let anyone forget what happened. *The Guardian* quotes him as saying at the time:

> My real disappointment was that he [Umaga] didn't come up as I was being stretchered off which I thought would just be a common courtesy between captains, whether he had been involved or not. I don't know whether that shows any element of guilt or not. At the time and post-match when I thought about it, that certainly disappointed me.

Opposite Prince William shakes hands with All Blacks captain Tana Umaga.
WILLIAM WEST/AFP VIA GETTY IMAGES

In some circumstances, this sort of thing would have a galvanising effect on a team. Unfortunately, as much as Campbell and Woodward tried to engineer one, the fuss made over the O'Driscoll incident had the totally opposite effect. Especially when Campbell collected up every negative reaction article from the New Zealand press and pinned them on a wall in the team hotel. The incident was now defining a tour that had already come under a serious amount of scrutiny due to the bloated size of the squad and management staff. 'Every day we are briefed on what we should and should not say. It becomes all-encompassing and a distraction,' said Dawson.

Campbell then gave a team talk, a duty usually only reserved for the coach or captain. To say that it didn't go down well is a serious understatement, and it's not hard to see that Woodward had clearly lost touch with his players if this was what he was resorting to. 'For reasons known only to Alastair, he thinks it is a good idea to compare our tour of duty with that of soldiers in Iraq,' said Dawson. 'He suggests we lack desire and tries to use the example of a theatre of war to put our situation into perspective.' As O'Connell recalled it, Campbell 'told us that in every campaign and every crisis, there comes a moment when the people in the thick of it realise they need to dig deep' but that 'he didn't get that feeling looking at us. He didn't have the sense that we were fighting back. Everyone's expression is one of disbelief. I am getting angry inside.'

It's important to note that not everyone felt that Campbell was a complete sideshow, though. O'Callaghan said that one of the main reasons he was unpopular was because there were 'English boys hung up over the political side from things they disagreed with that Tony Blair had done. It is hard to get beyond that. They say don't talk about religion and politics, and there you have one of the main men in it.'

The Lions felt as though they were under siege moving into the next test in Wellington. This was to be make or break, and the interest in the series had reached fever pitch because by now there were 30,000 fans that had travelled from the UK to support their team. It's highly unlikely that any of them would have been aware of the turmoil going on behind the scenes, yet even if they had been, it's unlikely that it would have dampened their enthusiasm. The red-clad horde filled every pub they came across and amped up each match with a massive injection of noise and atmosphere. Despite the team performing poorly, this was why Lions tours were so treasured by fans of the game in both hemispheres.

Half of Westpac Stadium was bathed in red for the second test, while home fans played their part and had half the stands wearing black. The Lions had a new captain, Welshman Gareth Thomas, who'd been handed one of the toughest assignments in sport because the All Blacks weren't just going to be better in the second test. They were going to hit the afterburners and put on one of the greatest performances of all time. Prince William, who at that stage was still sporting a full head of hair, had flown down to New Zealand to be in attendance. 'The New Zealand team that year, I don't think there's a team on the planet that would have got close to them. They had players

right on their form that coped under pressure,' Thomas said afterwards.

Thomas instructed his men to face the haka in the more traditional manner for the Wellington test. After renditions of 'God Defend New Zealand' and 'The Power of Four', the Lions simply lined up shoulder to shoulder on their own 10-metre line and watched Gear lead 'Ka Mate' again. The noise from their supporters was deafening, drowning out the kaea even though he had a set of microphones pointed at him to amplify the haka through the stadium's loudspeakers.

Despite the torrent of points that was to come, the Lions actually started the second test as the much better team. They essentially did what the All Blacks had done to them in the first test, but even better—breaking upfield in the first minute and creating a gap for Thomas to score the first try. It was a rapid start. Unbelievably, they were looking highly likely to score again not long after when Dwayne Peel also broke upfield and drew a penalty. Wilkinson's shot at goal hit the post and bounced back into the field of play, but the chase was perfect by Jason Robinson and they contested the breakdown well, deep inside the All Blacks' 22. Then O'Callaghan, whose two-metre frame was obviously too big to slow down as he got close to the ruck, launched himself off his feet right in front of the referee and connected mid-air with Rodney So'oialo.

That move essentially doomed the Lions, because they didn't touch the ball again in the All

Opposite Gareth Thomas is welcomed to the field in the third and final test.
ROSS LAND/GETTY IMAGES

Blacks' 22 for a long, long time. Dan Carter took control from that point, setting up a try for none other than Umaga after 17 minutes. After all the talk during the week about their skipper, it was the perfect riposte from a New Zealand point of view—the ultimate 'actions speak louder than words' moment. Not long afterwards, Sivivatu scored from a standing start out wide. Carter's virtuoso moment came after half-time when he found himself out on the wing, so put a kick along the deck that sat up perfectly for him to dive on in the corner. The first five ripped through the Lions again to score his second with 10 minutes to go, then Richie McCaw put an exclamation point on the performance to make the final score 48–18. Just to rub it in, the All Blacks played the last few minutes with only 14 men as they'd used all their subs when Carter came off with a shoulder injury.

It was the All Blacks' highest score against the Lions in over a century of them coming to New Zealand. As well as Carter's seminal performance, another enduring memory was of Woodward slowly turning and walking up the Westpac Stadium tunnel after the final whistle, wondering how on earth he'd got it so wrong.

There was still one more test to play, at Eden Park, which has become more of a footnote to the 2005 Lions tour than anything else. However, Carter's injury meant that he didn't even play, so there were some hopes that the tourists could salvage something out of what was already being dubbed the most disastrous Lions series ever. Unfortunately, for most of the squad, minds had already started focusing on the flight home. Flanker Lewis Moody remembered 'that last week being a totally different affair to the rest of the tour. It seemed everyone had switched off.' It showed when the team took the field for their last test. They were whipped again, 38–19, which still flattered the Lions' performance. The Lions left New Zealand with their tails firmly between their legs, amid serious questions about whether this might be the last time we'd ever see the composite side tour in the professional era.

Yet, upon reflection, the 2005 Lions tour wasn't the complete disgrace that it has often been labelled. The midweek side won all their games, which reflected well on their coach, the extremely popular Scotsman Ian McGeechan. They drew massive crowds wherever they went, and showed that New Zealand had what it took to be able to host a World Cup in the future. Moreover, it was a return to the days when a rugby tour could completely take over the national consciousness and rally the population behind the All Blacks. The Lions themselves learned some valuable lessons as to what not to do, which would come in very handy the next time they took the field.

Sir Clive Woodward's rugby coaching career ended with the series loss. He made an ill-fated venture into football, serving as high-performance manager at Southampton FC for two months before resigning. He now serves as a commentary pundit for the *Daily Mail* and has gained a reputation for being incredibly critical of the English national side. The tour also marked the end of Alastair Campbell's brief career as a sports media adviser. He returned to journalism and politics, recently ending up on the losing side of the Brexit battle.

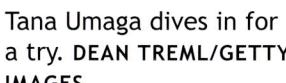

Tana Umaga dives in for a try. DEAN TREML/GETTY IMAGES

Donncha O'Callaghan was selected for the Lions again four years later. He kept playing professional rugby until 2018, when he retired at the age of 39. Matt Dawson earned the ire of New Zealanders in 2015 by appearing to mock the haka on a TV advert for an Italian clothing label. Tana Umaga and Brian O'Driscoll were seen together in a post on the Irish Rugby Football Union's official Instagram in 2018, engaging in a hongi as a symbolic showing that they had put the spear-tackle incident behind them.

In 2009, the British & Irish Lions defied the doom merchants and set out on a tour to South Africa. McGeechan was given the head coaching job this time around. The series is remembered as one of the most pulsating ever played, with the Lions only just losing the first two tests before comfortably winning the third. Better was to come in 2013, when the Lions won a series against the Wallabies, their first since 1997.

But it was their return to New Zealand in 2017 that really restored the Lions' mana. This time, there was no spread-out formation to face the haka. No spin doctor. No 'The Power of Four'. They lost the first test against the All Blacks but scored one of the best tries ever seen on Eden Park, then regrouped to win the second test in Wellington. Then, in one of the most dramatic finishes to a series ever, the two sides drew the last test 15-all and shared the honours.

'It is always an honour, I respect the haka, it gets you pumped up watching them do it live in front of you. It's amazing, it's an amazing experience.'
—MANU TUILAGI, ENGLAND CENTRE

**26 October 2019
Yokohama International Stadium, Yokohama**

All Blacks 7
(Ardie Savea try; Richie Mo'unga con)

England 19
(Manu Tuilagi try; George Ford 4 pen, Owen Farrell con)

All Blacks

15 Beauden Barrett
14 Sevu Reece
13 Jack Goodhue
12 Anton Lienert-Brown
11 George Bridge
10 Richie Mo'unga
9   Aaron Smith
8   Kieran Read (c)
7   Ardie Savea
6   Scott Barrett
5   Sam Whitelock
4   Brodie Retallick
3   Nepo Laulala
2   Codie Taylor
1   Joe Moody

Reserves

16 Dane Coles
17 Ofa Tuungafasi
18 Angus Ta'avao
19 Patrick Tuipulotu
20 Sam Cane
21 TJ Perenara
22 Sonny Bill Williams
23 Jordie Barrett

England

15 Elliot Daly
14 Anthony Watson
13 Manu Tuilagi
12 Owen Farrell (c)
11 Jonny May
10 George Ford
9   Ben Youngs
8   Billy Vunipola
7   Sam Underhill
6   Tom Curry
5   Courtney Lawes
4   Maro Itoje
3   Kyle Sinckler
2   Jamie George
1   Mako Vunipola

Reserves

16 Luke Cowan-Dickie
17 Joe Marler
18 Dan Cole
19 George Kruis
20 Mark Wilson
21 Willi Heinz
22 Henry Slade
23 Jonathan Joseph

The England team face the haka before the Rugby World Cup semi-final.
RICHARD HEATHCOTE/WORLD RUGBY VIA GETTY IMAGES

THE PINCER

Opposite Owen Farrell smirks as the All Blacks perform the haka. LYNNE CAMERON/GETTY IMAGES

England's head coach Eddie Jones during the pre-match warm-up, aware that his players have got something cooked up in response to the haka. ASHLEY WESTERN/MB MEDIA/GETTY IMAGES

WHEN TWO PROUD RUGBY nations clash, the pressure is always intense. Players run out of the tunnel with the weight of millions of fans on their shoulders, knowing that one mistake or moment of brilliance could make or break their chances. And when that match happens to be a Rugby World Cup knockout clash, the pressure amps up to another level. It's all-consuming. You can feel it in the air.

A long-held mantra of the All Blacks has been to walk towards the pressure, but where do you walk when pressure is all around you? That is exactly how England wanted the All Blacks to feel when they performed the haka prior to the 2019 Rugby World Cup semi-final in Yokohama. This wasn't just any semi-final, though. This was perhaps the most anticipated semi-final in Rugby World Cup history.

Both the All Blacks and England had waltzed through their respective pools unbeaten before demolishing their quarter-final opponents. The All Blacks laid waste to Ireland in a sublime 46–14 performance. Ireland had beaten the All Blacks twice in recent years and were meant to push the men in black close. On this occasion, Ireland had no answer as the All Blacks racked up seven tries in a breathtaking display of attacking rugby.

England were equally impressive in defeating

THE PINCER / 183

Opposite top Referee Nigel Owens attempts to pull back the England team as they cross over halfway. DAVID ROGERS/GETTY IMAGES

Opposite below English players stand tall as they flank the haka. HANDOUT/ WORLD RUGBY VIA GETTY IMAGES

Australia to claim their spot in the final four. After leading by just one point early in the second half, England swarmed Australia on defence and stretched them on attack to romp to a 40–16 victory and secure their first Rugby World Cup semi-final berth in 12 years.

The stage was set. A Rugby World Cup semi-final between the two form teams of the tournament at a capacity Yokohama International Stadium.

Renowned for his mind games and pre-match strategy, England coach Eddie Jones spent the week leading up to the semi-final heaping the pressure on the reigning champions. 'New Zealand talk about walking towards pressure. Well this week the pressure is going to be chasing them down the street,' quipped Jones. 'The busiest bloke in Tokyo will be Gilbert Enoka, their mental skills coach.'

With Jones determinedly playing the underdog card, the world's press naturally turned their attention and headlines to an All Blacks side pursuing an unprecedented third straight Rugby World Cup title. 'We know we are under pressure; we don't need Eddie to tell us that,' All Blacks coach Steve Hansen told a media conference on the eve of the highly anticipated clash.

And then the time for talking was done.

Over 73,000 fans crammed into Yokohama International Stadium on Saturday 26 October 2019 to witness a match that many pundits were calling the real Rugby World Cup final. The stadium that was eerily tranquil just hours earlier suddenly transformed into a cauldron of noise as the All Blacks strode forward to perform 'Kapa O Pango'. No one foresaw what was coming next.

England, who were required by World Rugby guidelines to stay behind the 40-metre line, advanced in a V formation over the halfway line and surrounded the All Blacks from left to right. Match officials attempted to push England back, but they stood their ground as TJ Perenara started to lead the under-siege challenge.

Accustomed to eyeballing a line of opponents standing shoulder to shoulder, the All Blacks' heads swivelled left and right, unsure where to look as 23 white jerseys engulfed them across the park. England captain Owen Farrell stayed in the middle of the formation, grinning as he stared down his opposite Kieran Read at the head of the haka.

This was psychological warfare. Premeditated and deliberate. An ambush that was in all likelihood masterminded by their wily coach.

The All Blacks completed their haka with all the usual passion and intensity you would expect for such a big occasion. But there was no post-haka staredown as they quickly turned to regroup, knowing that England had just thrown the first curve ball of what promised to be an epic contest.

England were under no illusions that they would face a World Rugby fine for breaking protocol, but their objective had been achieved. They had dialled up the pressure on the All Blacks and accepted the challenge. Now it was game on.

The opening two minutes of the semi-final belonged to England and set the platform for the match. After a sharp break by fullback Elliot Daly, the England pack battered the All Blacks' line before Manu Tuilagi dived over for the

Manu Tuilagi of England crosses for a try after only a minute and a half of play.
CAMERON SPENCER/GETTY IMAGES

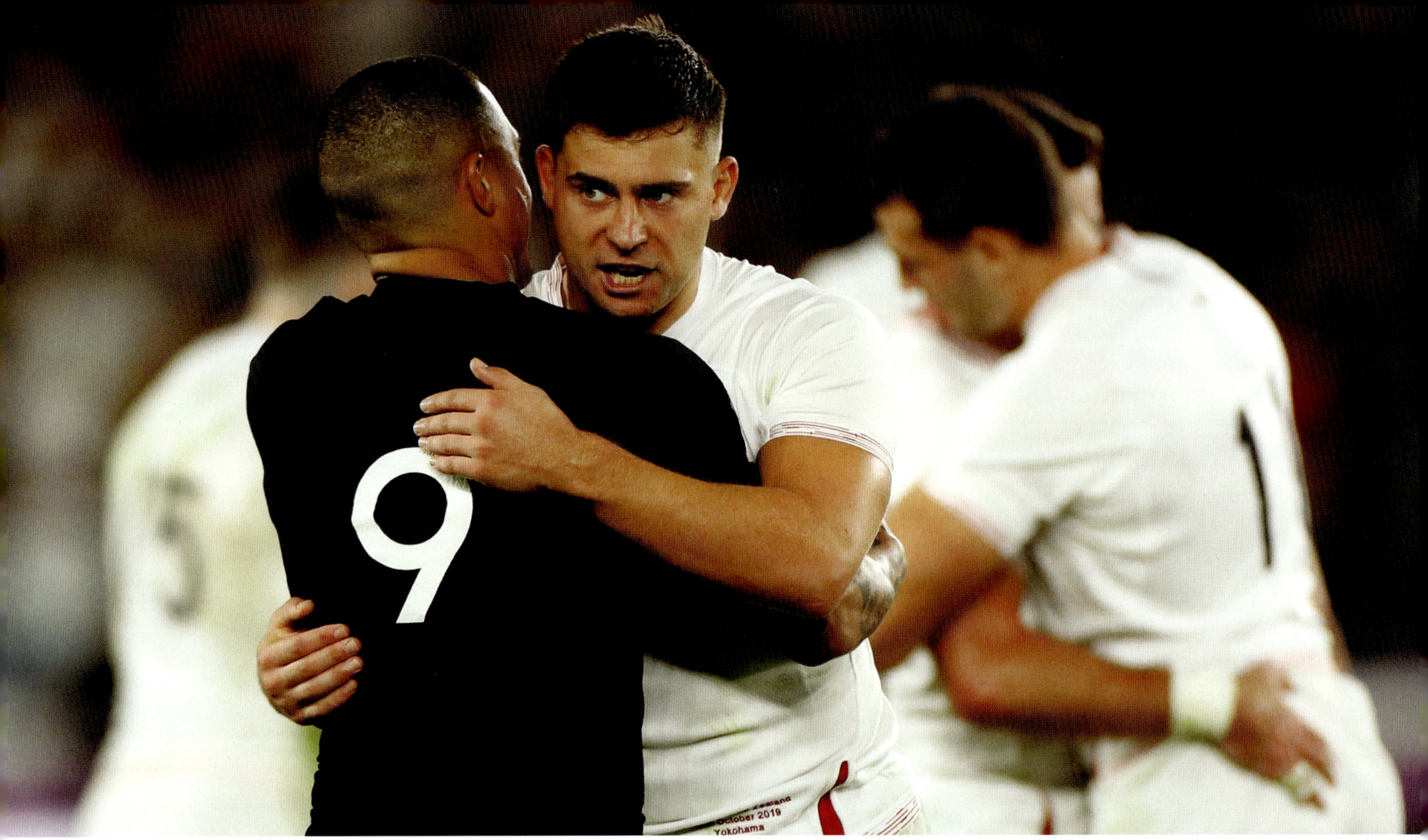
October 2019
Yokohama
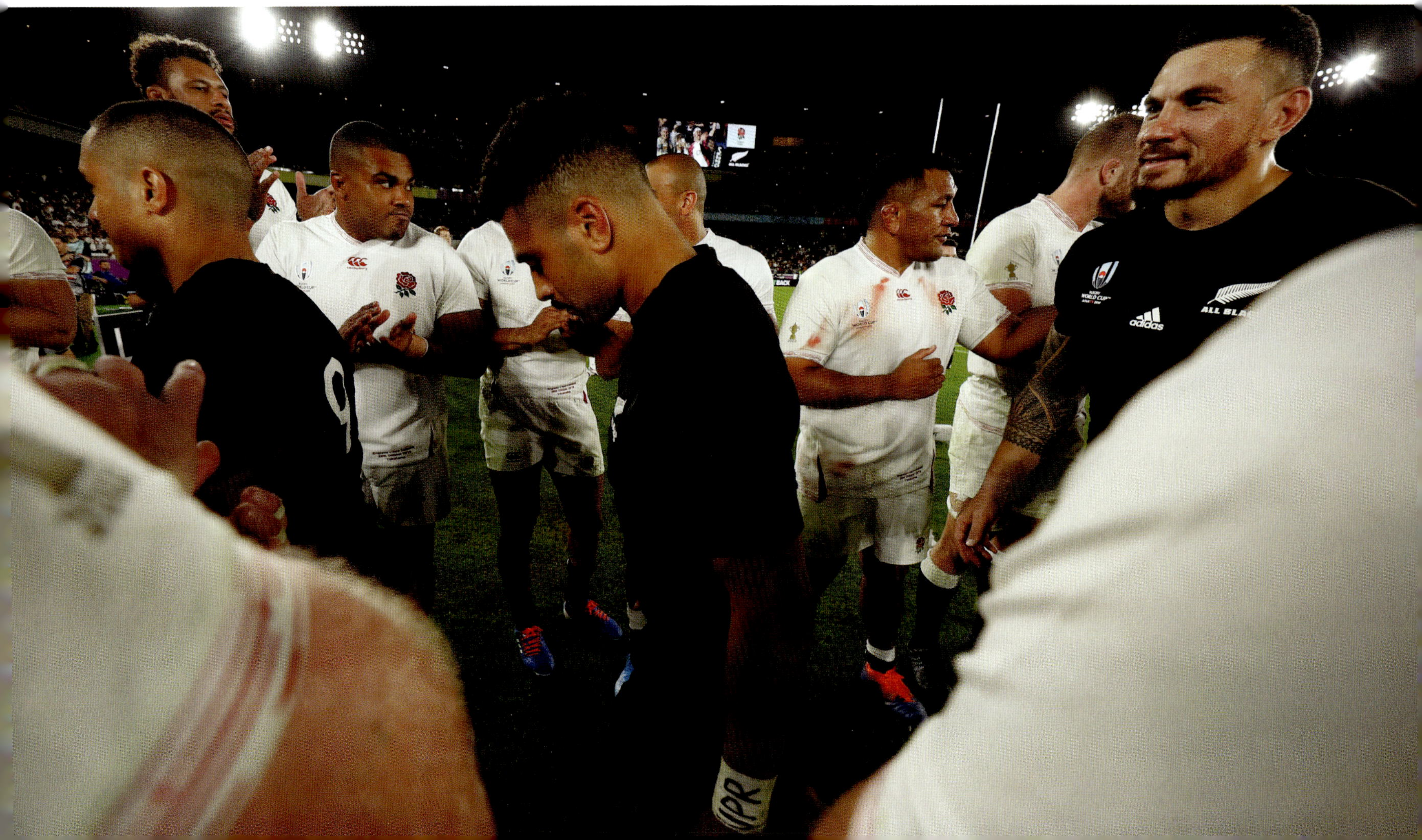
adidas

Opposite top Aaron Smith congratulates Ben Youngs. HANNAH PETERS/GETTY IMAGES

Opposite below The All Blacks file off the field at Yokohama International Stadium, their World Cup dreams shattered. HANNAH PETERS/GETTY IMAGES

opening strike. It was a telling blow early in the game, and one from which the All Blacks never recovered. England maintained their intensity for the full 80 minutes and forced the All Blacks into uncharacteristic mistakes. The All Blacks' dynamic attack was smothered by an unrelenting wall of white.

It was a masterclass in knockout rugby from England. In the end, the final score of 19–7 flattered the All Blacks. They had been outplayed in almost every department and could have lost by a bigger margin had England not had two tries disallowed either side of the half-time break.

England centre Tuilagi was a titan during the semi-final and said that the haka was something he always looked forward to facing: 'For me I think it is the fifth time I have played the All Blacks. It is always an honour, I respect the haka, it gets you pumped up watching them do it live in front of you. It's amazing, it's an amazing experience.' He added that England planned their response to show the All Blacks that they were up for the challenge and would not roll over. 'Everyone wanted to show that we were ready and together. It was something different that I think Eddie [Jones] suggested.'

As expected, England were fined for crossing the halfway line and public opinion was divided on whether the haka had been disrespected or not, although All Blacks coach Steve Hansen didn't believe so, commenting post-match:

> I thought their response was fantastic. They didn't get fined for responding [the way] they did, they got fined because they went over the halfway. Everyone knows you're not allowed to come over the halfway. If you understand the haka, then [you know] the haka requires a response. It is a challenge to you personally and it requires you to have a response. I thought it was brilliant, quite imaginative too. It was to accept the challenge and be ready to take the All Blacks head on.

One man who definitely took that approach literally was English centre Tuilagi, who told media afterwards that for him, the game started with the haka itself: 'Playing the All Blacks, you can't wait. They're the best team in the world. You need to attack them right from the start.'

THE LOST HAKA

Opposite Cliff Porter leads the All Blacks side out to play against Devon in 1924.
NZ RUGBY MUSEUM

29 November 1924
St Helen's Ground, Swansea

All Blacks 19
(William Irvine 2, Maurice Brownlie, Ken Svenson tries; Mark Nicholls 2 con, pen)

Wales 0

All Blacks

- FB George Nepia
- W   Jack Steel
- C   Bert Cooke
- C   Mark Nicholls
- W   Ken Svenson
- FH Neil McGregor
- SH Jimmy Mill
- WF Jim Parker
- F   Les Cupples
- L   Cyril Brownlie
- F   Jock Richardson (c)
- L   Read Masters
- L   Maurice Brownlie
- P   William Irvine
- P   Quentin Donald

Wales

- FB Codger Johnson
- W   Rowe Harding
- C   Bert Stock
- C   Albert Jenkins
- W   Ernie Finch
- FH Eddie Williams
- SH Bobby Delahay
- N8 Jack Wetter (c)
- F   Douglas Marsden-Jones
- F   Dai Hiddlestone
- L   Dai Parker
- L   Steve Morris
- P   Charlie Pugh
- H   Jack Gore
- P   Cliff Williams

NOTE: In this era jersey numbers were often random, and positions had not yet been standardised across the world. New Zealand rugby still favoured the 2-3-2 scrum formation, so this team included three locks and an extra 'wing forward'.

The All Blacks challenge the Combined Services side at Twickenham. NZ RUGBY MUSEUM

Instead of the actual translation being printed . . . headlines read that the haka meant something along the lines of: 'Now we are in England! Feed us! Feed us! Or we will tear you! Tear you! Tear you!'

THE 1924-25 ALL BLACKS own a special place in the history of not only New Zealand rugby but also the game itself. Their goal on the tour was to avenge the one blemish on the record of their predecessors, the 1905 Originals, with a win against Wales in Cardiff. But the 1924 side ended up doing much, much better than that when they became the first All Blacks side to go through an entire tour of the UK with a perfect record, winning 32 straight matches—with a few in France and British Columbia on the way home thrown in for good measure. They truly earned their tag of the 'Invincibles'.

But while their on-field deeds and the names of George Nepia, the Brownlie brothers and Mark Nicholls have passed into the pantheon of All Blacks greats, there is another aspect to this side that ties them to the team of today. Like those before them, this All Blacks team performed the haka before their matches. However, that haka was not 'Ka Mate' but a new version composed specifically for the team. It's one that looks awfully familiar to anyone who has watched the team play an important test match in the twenty-first century, but was written on the sort of journey that would never be undertaken these days.

The All Blacks left home on 25 July 1924, with the ink still fresh on the newspapers asserting that they were the worst team to ever represent the country. This seems a little harsh in hindsight, but they had lost a match to New South Wales in Sydney, then went down to Auckland on their return. The team embarked on the RMS *Remuera* for a 35-day voyage that would take them across the Pacific Ocean, and they tried to maintain match fitness by training on the ship's deck. That didn't always go well, according to Canterbury lock Read Masters in his book *With the All Blacks in Great Britain, France, Canada & Australia 1924–5*:

> Many of the boys suffered injuries through falling on the hard decks . . . sometimes as many as seven were excused duty altogether. Fortunately there was only one bad injury, and that happened when Jack Steel crashed into the bulwarks and seriously injured his forearm, which for some days was thought to be broken. It really was a miracle that worse accidents did not occur, when a scrum would collapse through the roll of the ship hurling some of us against the iron bulwarks or deckhouses.

The ship made its way east, stopping off at Pitcairn Island to buy fruit off the tiny population. Somewhere between there and the Panama Canal,

Opposite Caricatures of the 1924 'Invincibles', including a seriously inaccurate translation of their unique haka.
NZ RUGBY MUSEUM

a couple of men accompanying the tour composed what would be the Invincibles' haka. Native Land Court judge Frank Acheson and Wiremu Rangi wrote down the haka and its actions, which were distributed to the team and practised on the rest of the voyage.

> *Kia whakangawari au i ahau!*
> *Hi aue . . . hi!*
>
> *Ko Niu Tirenu e ngunguru nei!*
> *Hi, au! Au! Aue, ha! Hi!*
> *Ko niu Tirenu e ngunguru nei!*
> *Hi, au! Au! Aue, ha! Hi!*
>
> *I ahaha!*
> *Ka tu te ihi*
>
> *Ihi ka tu te wanawana*
> *Ki runga i te rangi, e tu iho nei, tu iho nei, hi!*

Sound familiar? It's almost exactly the same as the first half of 'Kapa O Pango', the haka the All Blacks debuted in 2005. The 1924 version had a second half, which was specifically paying tribute to the British Isles and their rugby prowess and hospitality.

> *Tena i poua! O rongo Ingarangi hau ana i te ao e*
> *A haha! Horahia mai o mahi ki ahau*
> *Horahia mai o tiima kaihau*
> *O mahi, aku mahi me hui*

> *Remain alert! The strength of England is known throughout the world*
> *Now then! Let us see what England can do*
> *Bring forth your strong teams*
> *Let us combine in friendly rivalry*
>
> *Nga mahi tinihanga me kiki*
> *Au au hei!*
>
> *Anything unsportsmanlike together we shall kick aside*
> *The strength of the kick*
>
> *A haha*
> *Ka mutu nga mahi haramai ki Tireni*
> *Au Au Aue ha!*
>
> *Now then!*
> *After the battles are over come to New Zealand*
> *It is ended!*

It was a very magnanimous gesture by the All Blacks, who were of course expecting to perform it for the crowd before every match. While the *Remuera* was making its way across the Atlantic, the words and meanings were telegraphed forward to an eager British press. It's there the story takes an unfortunately familiar turn. Instead of the actual translation being printed in the Home newspapers, headlines read that the haka meant something along the lines of: 'Now we are in England! Feed us! Feed us! Or we will tear you! Tear you! Tear you!'

Performing the haka against Cornwall before the second match of the tour.
NZ RUGBY MUSEUM

Masters recounted that the (probably deliberate) tabloid mangling of what was supposed to be a way of honouring their opposition and hosts was an unfortunate introduction to the tour:

> Some girls in London treated the matter as a joke, and sent us packets of biscuits stating they were quite prepared to feed us, as long as we didn't tear them to pieces. There is not the slightest doubt that this misinterpretation had the effect of prejudicing some people against our haka, which was resented in some quarters.

While that resentment existed, the haka was still a very popular part of the All Blacks' impressive tour. There's newsreel footage on YouTube of it being performed, which shows a methodical and well-rehearsed All Blacks team very much taking the matter seriously, performing the actions in unison and with a look of determination in their eyes. As was the custom, they faced the grandstand while their opposition watched on curiously from behind them.

It was a part of all but two matches, and on those occasions the press criticised the All Blacks for not performing it—so, like today, it seemed as though the All Blacks couldn't win, no matter what they did, in the eyes of some British journalists.

On the field, though, winning was all they did. From the first match against Devon right through to the last game against Victoria (Canada), the All Blacks walked off the field knowing that the beer was going to taste extra good that night. Ireland

THE LOST HAKA / 199

While the Invincibles had their own haka in 1924, that's not quite where the story ends. Evidence of yet another haka from that year surfaced in 2012, in a typed-out version of a very different haka, which was property of Invincibles winger Gus Hart. The letterhead of the sheet that it is written on is from the Huddart Parker shipping line, which indicates that it was from the All Blacks' preliminary tour of Australia prior to them leaving for the UK. Handwritten on the document are the words: 'This is the All Blacks' Maori haka.' There is no footage of it being performed on that tour, so the haka detailed in Hart's sheet will likely remain a mystery.

NZ RUGBY MUSEUM

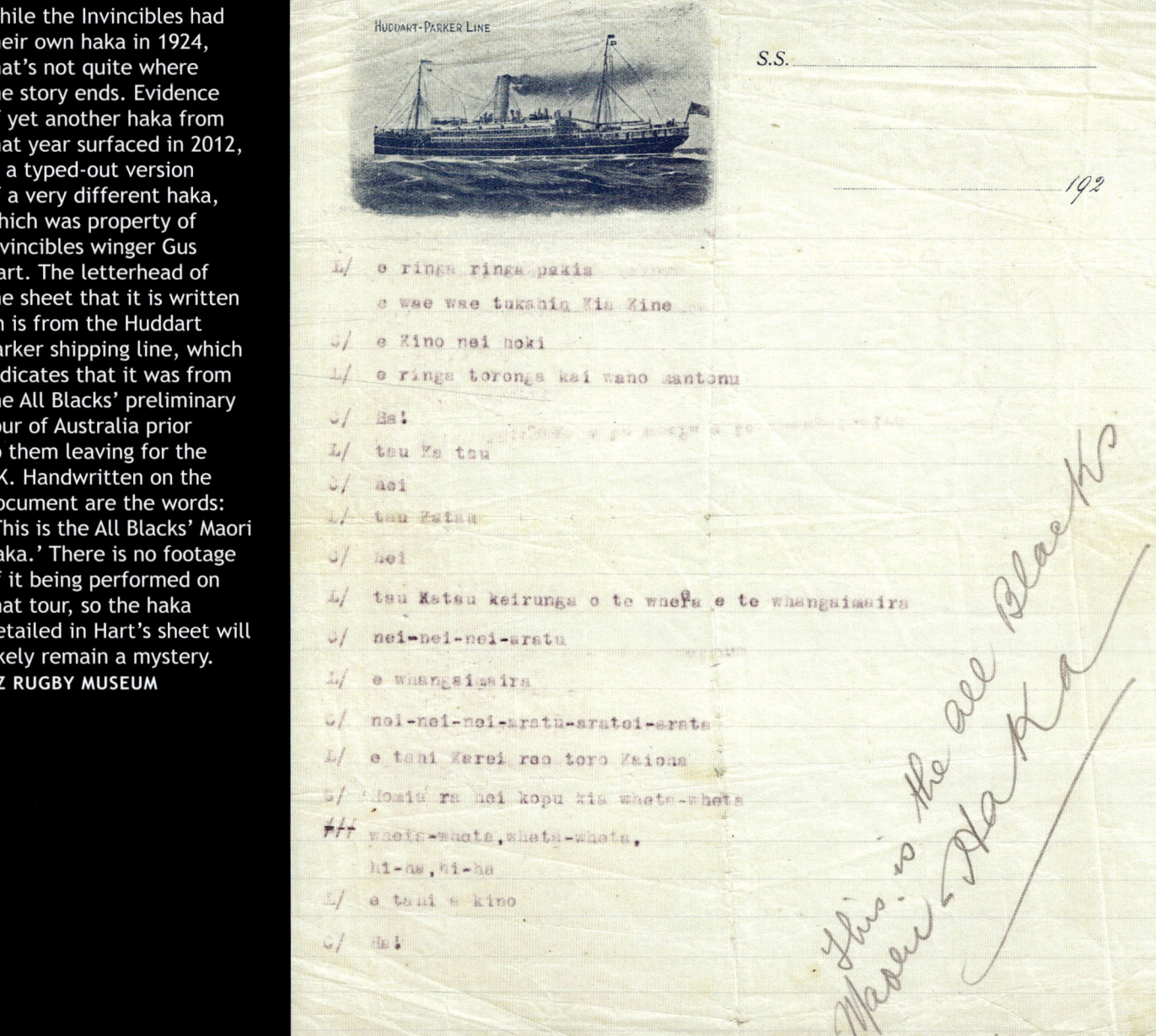

Below The timing was a bit off in the haka before the Leicester game. NZ RUGBY MUSEUM

were beaten 6–0 in Dublin and England were swept away 17–11 by an All Blacks side reduced to 14 men for all but 10 minutes of the game after Cyril Brownlie became the first man ever to be sent off in a test match. That scoreline greatly flattered the English, who were outscored four tries to two but were never in the game thanks to a fired-up performance from Cyril's brother Maurice, who scored a try.

In between those two tests, the Invincibles got what they'd travelled over the oceans for. The date of 29 November in Swansea was chosen for the revenge match against Wales, who didn't help themselves by mockingly performing a parody haka of their own. The laugh they got was the last positive reaction from the 50,000-strong crowd, though. The All Blacks dominated the game from start to finish, with Maurice Brownlie opening the scoring with a rampaging try. Welsh captain Jack Wetter picked up a leg injury after a hit from Nepia. William 'Bull' Irvine, a Wairarapa prop, scored the first of his two tries as the All Blacks increasingly bullied their hosts into a physical game. Wellington winger Ken 'Snowy' Svenson added another in the second half, before Irvine collected a kick-through to score under the posts and complete the rout.

Job done: All Blacks 19, Wales 0.

THE LOST HAKA / 201

FACING THE BLACK FERNS

Opposite The Black Ferns face off with England before the 2017 Rugby World Cup final in Belfast.
CHARLES MCQUILLAN/WORLD RUGBY VIA GETTY IMAGES

**17 June 2017
Rotorua International Stadium, Rotorua**

Black Ferns 21
(Kendra Cocksedge, Portia Woodman, Victoria Subritzsky-Nafatali tries; Kendra Cocksedge 3 con)

England 29
(Emily Scarratt, Abbie Scott, Lydia Thompson, Marlie Packer, Vicky Fleetwood tries; Emily Scarratt 2 con)

Black Ferns	England
15 Selica Winiata	15 Danielle Waterman
14 Portia Woodman	14 Lydia Thompson
13 Stacey Waaka	13 Emily Scarratt
12 Chelsea Alley	12 Rachael Burford
11 Renee Wickliffe	11 Kay Wilson
10 Kelly Brazier	10 Katy McLean
9 Kendra Cocksedge	9 Natasha Hunt
8 Linda Itunu	8 Sarah Hunter (c)
7 Sarah Goss	7 Marlie Packer
6 Rawinia Everitt	6 Alex Matthews
5 Charmaine Smith	5 Abbie Scott
4 Eloise Blackwell	4 Tamara Taylor
3 Aldora Itunu	3 Sarah Bern
2 Fiao'o Fa'amausili (c)	2 Amy Cokayne
1 Toka Natua	1 Rochelle Clark

Reserves

16 Te Kura Ngata-Aerengamate	16 Vicky Fleetwood
17 Sosoli Talawadua	17 Vickii Cornborough
18 Aleisha Nelson	18 Justine Lucas
19 Rebecca Wood	19 Harriet Millar-Mills
20 Charmaine McMenamin	20 Izzy Noel-Smith
21 Kristina Sue	21 La Toya Mason
22 Victoria Subritzsky-Nafatali	22 Amber Reed
23 Honey Hireme	23 Emily Scott

The Black Ferns perform the haka in Rotorua. ANDREW CORNAGA/PHOTOSPORT

'I grew up in a rugby-mad family. The haka's so iconic, so when we'd watch the All Blacks it meant that we'd be sat down 10 minutes before kick-off because we had to watch that part. To be honest, when I was younger I never thought I'd end up facing it.'

—EMILY SCARRATT, 2019 WORLD RUGBY WOMEN'S PLAYER OF THE YEAR

IT WAS A BIG day in Rotorua. The city had swollen with an influx of rugby fans from around the Bay of Plenty, and plenty more from even further afield. There was a double-header on at the grandly named International Stadium, so the bar district down on 'Eat Street' had been heaving since before noon. The Black Ferns were due to play England in the first match, followed by the British & Irish Lions against the Māori All Blacks later on. As the rain began to fall outside in the late afternoon, Emily Scarratt and her English side prepared themselves in the ageing changing rooms.

'The hype around the game, the hype around the country was massive,' Scarratt said in March of 2020, in the midst of the Women's Six Nations Championship. 'There were loads of people supporting—we even had some fans that we normally wouldn't with the Welsh, Scottish and Irish there to follow the Lions. It was quite strange for us as English people.'

With a World Cup looming in just a couple of months, Scarratt knew that a big performance on New Zealand soil would send a message that they would be a serious threat at the business end of the season. The 1.81-metre-tall fullback/centre had been wearing the English jersey for almost a decade, after debuting as an 18-year-old. Women's rugby had come an awfully long way since Scarratt had grown up watching mostly men's teams play on TV as a girl in Leicester, such that by the time of this match there had been five official Women's Rugby World Cups—four of which had been won by the team down the hall.

In that Black Ferns' changing room, reserve hooker Te Kura Ngata-Aerengamate was taping up and getting ready to head out to face one of the stiffest tests of her career. But she was also readying herself for the team's haka: 'Ko Uhia Mai'—'Let It Be Known'. '[It's] like a rumbling in your heart. You get into this zone of extra energy, like you're on the next level,' Ngata-Aerengamate told Britain's *The Daily Telegraph* in 2017.

> For me, it's like I'm getting my second wind before the game has even started. You feel so fired up; it's like you've had some sort of upper that gets you really going. It's an adrenalin rush. I remember being up in my room the other day and just tearing up thinking about when I do the haka, my ancestors are spiritually behind me. I could really feel the spiritual side of it and just how wicked it felt. It is like having super powers.

Soon, the teams were out on the wet field. The English lined up on their 10-metre line, while

Opposite top Scarratt fends off New Zealand's Selica Winiata during the Rugby Super Series match in Rotorua. DAVID DAVIES/PA IMAGES VIA GETTY IMAGES

Opposite below England celebrate after their victory over the Black Ferns in front of a big Rotorua crowd. DAVID ROGERS/GETTY IMAGES

their opposition formed up for the challenge. 'It's always amazing facing it, how the crowd falls silent and tunes in,' said Scarratt, although that's not a sentiment shared by all of her teammates. 'People approach it in different ways. Some people rise up, some try not to get wrapped up in it. I always enjoy facing off against it—it's definitely something that gets me going.'

Whatever the English team did, it worked. They stunned the Black Ferns with a try after only a couple of minutes, scored by Scarratt after she'd pierced the midfield defence and slid over in the corner. 'It was a really good game. Whenever we play New Zealand, we know it's going to be really tough—we got off to a good start but it really yo-yoed from then on.'

It certainly did, with two of the biggest names in the Black Ferns hitting back to put them in front. First, halfback Kendra Cocksedge scored off a sweet chip and chase from 40 metres out, and then Scarratt's day went from great to garbage when she picked the worst person on the Black Ferns to throw an intercept to. After breaking the line with a powerful run, Scarratt tried a miracle offload that was snapped up by Portia Woodman. The former Northern Mystics netballer and now rugby superstar was untouched as she took the ball 70 metres in the other direction to score under the posts.

For New Zealand rugby fans, it seemed as though normal transmission had resumed and the all-conquering Black Ferns would run away with the game. However, the English took a leaf out of their male counterparts' tactics book when playing the All Blacks and kept the ball in tight. By half-time, they'd locked the score back up with a textbook lineout-drive try to lock Abbie Scott. Then, after the break, came the decisive score when winger Lydia Thompson fended off an uncharacteristically weak Woodman tackle to dive over in the corner. 'A lot of things worked for us, we kicked really well in that game. We kept New Zealand under pressure in terms of territory,' said Scarratt.

From there, England never looked back. Roared on by the big British contingent that had made their way to the stadium (and for the first half, the Lions squad themselves), they scored two more tries to push the lead out to an insurmountable 15 points as the clock ticked down. Although Victoria Subritzky-Nafatali tacked on a consolation try for the Black Ferns with a couple of minutes to go, England closed out a memorable victory on New Zealand soil—their first in 16 years. The side completed a lap of honour to the applause of both the home crowd and their newfound supporters from the three other nations of the United Kingdom. 'To have that win away in New Zealand, especially the nature of it, we look back on it with super-fond memories,' said Scarratt. 'With everything else that was going on with the Lions and the fans, it really was a once-in-a-lifetime opportunity.'

The evening got even better for the team, as after they showered and headed up to the stands, they got to watch the British & Irish Lions side

Opposite top Toka Natua dives over for one of her three tries. INPHO/DAN SHERIDAN/PHOTOSPORT

Opposite below Fiao'o Faamausili, Black Ferns captain, raises the silverware after the team's victory in the final of the 2017 Women's Rugby World Cup. DAVID ROGERS/GETTY IMAGES

comprehensively beat the Māori All Blacks 32–10. It had been a great moment for Scarratt and her English side, but the Black Ferns were already planning their revenge. Just two months later, the two sides lined up to face one another again, this time at the World Cup final in Belfast.

THE BLACK FERNS HAD demolished everyone on their way to the Women's Rugby World Cup final, scoring 258 points and only conceding 29. Portia Woodman managed the amazing feat of eight tries in a single game against the hapless Hong Kong, who were dispatched 121–0. Emily Scarratt's England side weren't too far off the pace, but went into the final at the Ravenhill ground as underdogs.

Everyone was expecting Woodman, who had scored 13 tries overall in the tournament, to dominate, but the Black Ferns found an unlikely try-scoring heroine in the form of Toka Natua. The loosehead prop had conceded a penalty try earlier in the game to the English, but more than made up for it with a remarkable hat-trick. Selica Winiata bagged a double, Kendra Cocksedge wriggled over, and Charmaine Smith smartly grounded the ball up against the goalpost pad to make the score 41–32 in what's been generally regarded as the greatest women's test match ever played. While the Black Ferns performed 'Ko Uhia Mai' after lifting the Cup, Scarratt and her England team were left ruing what might have been.

> It was a tough one for us. I remember afterwards having to tell the media that they were just better. It was high scoring, both sides scored some fantastic tries, but they just managed to control the little bits a bit better than we did. Towards the end of the game we just couldn't get the ball back off them when we really needed it. Sometimes you just have to put your hand up and say the better team won on the day.

There was a silver lining, though. Because of the highly entertaining nature of the game, the profile of women's rugby in the UK benefited immensely.

> So many people watched that game, they saw what a fantastic spectacle it was. We got a lot more fans off the back of that game—it wasn't a six-all stalemate, it was open rugby with tries being scored. Obviously you want to win the World Cup final, but we wanted to put on a show as well. It's really important that our games attract new viewers.

THE
INDLAMU

Opposite Werner Greeff introduces Doug Howlett to the Kings Park turf. ROSS LAND/GETTY IMAGES

10 August 2002
Kings Park, Durban

All Blacks 30
(Doug Howlett, Leon MacDonald, Aaron Mauger tries, penalty try; Andrew Mehrtens 2 pen, 2 con)

Springboks 23
(Neil de Kock, Andre Pretorius tries; Pretorius 2 pen, 2 con, dropped goal)

All Blacks	Springboks
15 Leon MacDonald	15 Werner Greeff
14 Doug Howlett	14 Breyton Paulse
13 Tana Umaga	13 Marius Joubert
12 Aaron Mauger	12 De Wet Barry
11 Caleb Ralph	11 Dean Hall
10 Andrew Mehrtens	10 Andre Pretorius
9 Justin Marshall	9 Neil de Kock
8 Scott Robertson	8 Bobby Skinstad
7 Richie McCaw	7 Joe van Niekerk
6 Reuben Thorne (c)	6 Corne Krige (c)
5 Simon Maling	5 AJ Venter
4 Chris Jack	4 Jannes Labuschagne
3 Greg Somerville	3 Willie Meyer
2 Tom Willis	2 James Dalton
1 Dave Hewett	1 Laurence Sephaka

Reserves

All Blacks	Springboks
16 Mark Hammett	16 Ollie le Roux
17 Joe McDonnell	17 Faan Rautenbach
18 Sam Broomhall	18 Victor Matfield
19 Marty Holah	19 Hendro Scholtz
20 Byron Kelleher	20 Bolla Conradie
21 Daryl Gibson	21 AJ Jacobs
22 Jonah Lomu	22 Brent Russell

Tana Umaga is taken in a high tackle by De Wet Barry, resulting in a controversial penalty try.
ROSS LAND/GETTY IMAGES

'This is no gimmick, it is a part of our rugby history and tradition.'
—JAKE WHITE, WORLD CUP-WINNING SPRINGBOKS COACH

HAKA IS A CHALLENGE, an honour and a show of respect. However, its roots lie in the oral knowledge transmission of Māori, a culture in which the tradition of the warrior is prevalent. Another culture whose people fought against the same colonial power, at the same time as Māori, lived half a world away in South Africa: the Zulu nation, which was engaged in the Anglo-Zulu War. They fought in formations known as 'impi'. The Zulu relied heavily on intimidation and noise to strike terror into the hearts of their opponents, with a combination of songs, chants and hammering their assegai (spears) on their mgobo (ox-hide shields). Their battle tactic, known as 'The Horns of the Bull', drew the enemy into a close-quarters fight. Their most stunning success came in 1879 when a Zulu army under King Cetshwayo wiped out a British force advancing into what is now the KwaZulu-Natal province in the Battle of Isandlwana.

So, it was fitting that when the first Springboks team began to tour the UK in 1906 and were expected to give a show of their homeland's culture to curious onlookers, the rugby side chose a Zulu indlamu (war cry). 'Ghee gammilio gshee' was described by a newspaper at the time as being:

> A fearsome thing. It is explained that when the Zulus rush into battle, etiquette does not allow the warriors to mention the name of the man about to be slain. However, as soon as the attacking party sets eyes on the wretched victim, the leader shouts out 'Gammilio!' which means 'that is his name!'; at the same time pointing at the victim with his spear, and thus the difficulty is overcome. The 'gshee' is meant to represent the hiss or whizz of the spear as it flies through the air.

The reception accorded to the Springboks' war cry was the same as to the haka, with warm appreciation from the crowd who sang in return. It's commonly thought that the performance of the indlamu ended before World War I, but that's not actually the case. The All Blacks and Springboks first met in a series in 1921, where the haka and indlamu faced off against one another. Admittedly, given the state of the All Blacks' haka at the time, it was more of an entertainment for the crowd than a torrid clash of two warrior cultures—which is why it was largely forgotten.

However, the next time the indlamu was performed against the All Blacks, it was led by Philip Nel in the 1928 series in South Africa. The debutant lock was born in Kranskop, only three hours away from Isandlwana, and spoke fluent Zulu. It's likely that Nel would have come into

The All Blacks perform their haka prior to the first test against the Springboks in 1921. **NZ RUGBY MUSEUM**

contact with actual veterans from the Battle of Isandlwana in his childhood.

One warrior nation against another, in a showdown of cultural challenges. The haka going up against a traditional indlamu should have been something that has been a part of rugby's greatest rivalry since its inception. But South Africa's complicated and disgraceful history of race relations meant that after World War II, the Springboks never performed the indlamu again. Apartheid dictated that a group of white men promoting the culture of an African nation was not going to be tolerated, and it's notable that the haka was not performed on the 1949 All Blacks tour of South Africa.

So that's where the Zulu pre-match challenge for the Springboks ends? Not quite.

Fast-forward a fair few decades and the All Blacks found themselves squaring up against their old foes at Kings Park, Durban, in the deciding match of the 2002 Tri Nations championship. It's a game that is remembered for one of the absolute worst moments in rugby history, when an overweight, drunk and incredibly bitter Boks supporter ran on to the field and assaulted referee David McHugh. It's a shame that this action is what sticks in everyone's memory, because before the kick-off the All Blacks came face to face with a combined impi of advancing Springboks and Zulu warriors.

The local Zulu group, armed with traditional assegai and mbogo, had performed for the crowd before the teams ran on to the field. This sort of celebration of local culture was nothing new in any part of the world. However, as the All Blacks formed up for 'Ka Mate', cheered on by the packed Kings Park crowd, the warriors flanked the Springboks. Their inDuna (leader), dressed in an elaborate leopard-skin headdress, positioned himself in front of the team. On his command, the Springboks moved forward over halfway to meet the challenge.

The effect was stunning. The South African crowd, who so often would greet the haka with a rendition of 'Olé, Olé, Olé', roared their approval at the impi's advance. The haka, led by Caleb Ralph, stood firm on the All Blacks' 10-metre line in the teeth of a snarling Springboks captain Corne Krige and the blades of the assegai.

The warriors charged off the field. The rugby battle was about to commence. The All Blacks side assembled that day by coach John Mitchell was stacked with the Super 12 champion Crusaders side, with 11 players in the starting XV and three more on the bench. The two sides had met once already that season, with the All Blacks coming away with a comprehensive 41–20 win in Wellington. This was followed by a narrow loss to the Wallabies in Sydney that meant the Bledisloe Cup stayed in Australia for the fifth season in a row. The Tri Nations was to be decided with this game, and the sun was shining down on the Kings Park pitch. This game was going to be a lung-buster, and the All Blacks had no problem with that because they ran the ball at a frenetic pace for the first minute and a half.

The problem was that the ball came flying out of a ruck, between Ralph's legs, and was pounced on by James Dalton. The Boks shifted the ball wide to winger Dean Hall and he outpaced the fractured defence to get an offload to Werner Greeff, who

in turn found Neil de Kock to score the opening try. Barely three minutes later, though, Andrew Mehrtens dummied his way through a gap and passed to Tana Umaga to set up Leon MacDonald for the All Blacks to strike back. It was a scintillating beginning to what would be a classic test match.

Then, the first moment of controversy. After Scott Robertson had charged down a Springboks clearance, Justin Marshall sent a 20-metre behind-the-back pass to a wide-open Aaron Mauger, who passed it on to Umaga. Desperately, De Wet Barry reached out and grabbed a handful of Umaga's face in a textbook high tackle. Referee David McHugh deemed it worthy of a penalty try, which incensed the South African fans, and rightly so. The problem was that a penalty try can be awarded if

Why do South African crowds sing 'Olé, Olé, Olé', a Spanish bullfighting song, almost exclusively in response to the haka? Evidence points to a mash-up song by South African comedian Leon Schuster released in 1995 called 'Champions', as part of an album to support the Springboks at that year's World Cup. The song contained the ubiquitous football chant (among a great many others) and caught on, ringing out over Ellis Park the day that South Africa won their first title. Ever since, 'Olé, Olé, Olé' has been a part of the All Blacks versus Springboks rivalry whenever matches are played in South Africa.

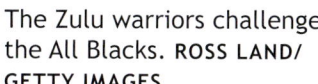

The Zulu warriors challenge the All Blacks. ROSS LAND/ GETTY IMAGES

you take the offending player out of the equation, yet while Barry's tackle was clearly illegal, there was nothing at all wrong with Marius Joubert's effort at exactly the same time. So, while the high shot should have been a penalty, it definitely didn't warrant the referee's extreme course of action.

Andre Pretorius pulled the Boks ahead after half an hour following another raid down the wing, ending with a chip and chase that eluded the All Blacks' cover defence. Umaga then again popped up as a crucial figure just before half-time, going through a gap on the Springboks' edge and popping a pass to a wide-open Doug Howlett to do what he did best 49 times in his career: run in a straight line down the wing and score a try: 17-all at half-time and the big crowd was watching a barnburner, as was a sizable chunk of New Zealanders tuning in at 3am local time.

The second half saw the second bit of aggravation for home fans. Breyton Paulse looked to have scored a crucial try, but McHugh rubbed it out because of a perceived obstruction. Somewhere high in the stands, an overweight 43-year-old in a very snugly fitting Springboks jersey decided he'd had enough of the Irishman's rulings and jumped the security fence surrounding the field. The man's name, Pieter van Zyl, was soon to become infamous around the rugby world, and perhaps his jersey helped camouflage his intent from the security guards. Van Zyl ran straight at McHugh and tackled him to the ground, only to be then set upon by players from both sides. When van Zyl was finally removed from the field, he had picked up a badly bloodied nose from someone dishing out a bit of extra-judicial punishment. It was one of the most ridiculous

THE INDLAMU / 221

Opposite top Richie McCaw and AJ Venter come to the ref's rescue. ROSS LAND/ GETTY IMAGES

Opposite below Pieter van Zyl is removed from the field by officials after assaulting Irish referee David McHugh. ROSS LAND/ GETTY IMAGES

Below Referee David McHugh is assisted from the field. ROSS LAND/GETTY IMAGES

intrusions ever seen on a rugby field, and McHugh cut a pitiful figure as he was helped from the pitch with a dislocated shoulder. He was replaced by Englishman Chris White, but that didn't give the Springboks the sort of help van Zyl would have hoped for. They only managed two more penalties, but the All Blacks sealed the win with a try to Mauger on the 70-minute mark.

It was the end to an epic test, which won the Tri Nations as well. Afterwards, van Zyl was completely unrepentant for his actions, claiming that it was the players who caused McHugh's injury. He was nonetheless convicted of assault and banned for life from attending any matches in South Africa.

Sadly, the impi that accompanied the Springboks onto the field that day to face the haka in Durban hasn't been seen since either. A group of warriors pumped up the crowd before another epic test in Cape Town in 2018, but there's been no further advance on a revival of the indlamu tradition from many years ago other than 2007 World Cup-winning coach Jake White calling for its return, saying, 'This is no gimmick, it is a part of our rugby history and tradition.'

To date, nothing has come of White's suggestion, but never say never. Siya Kolisi became the first black African to lift the Rugby World Cup in 2019, heralding yet another positive chapter in the integration of a sport that used to be a bastion of apartheid. Maybe one day the indlamu will return to challenge the haka.

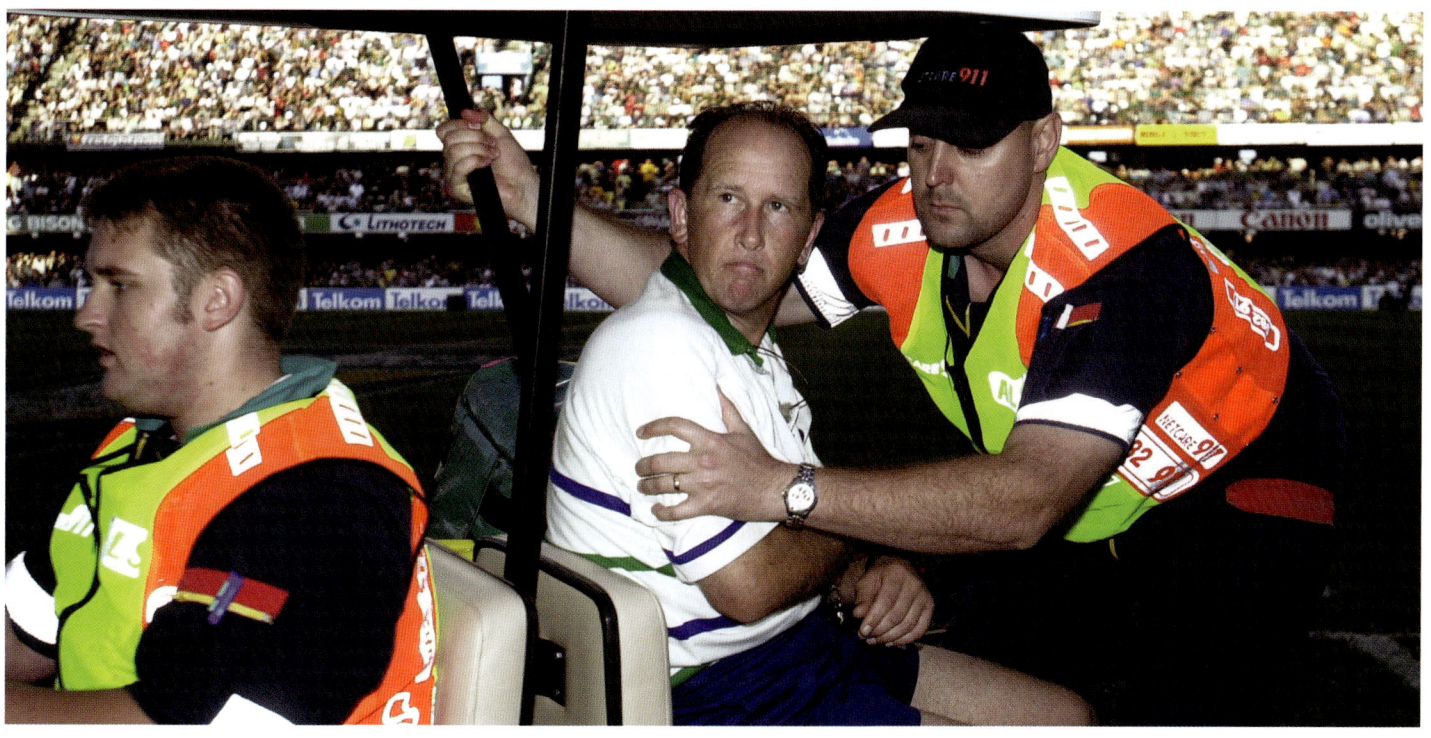

TE TĪMATANGA FOR AN IRISH ICON

Opposite Māori All Blacks players Ash Dixon (right) and Matt Proctor present a shirt in memory of former Munster coach Anthony Foley before the friendly between the two sides at Thomond Park. **STEPHEN POND/GETTY IMAGES**

11 November 2016
Thomond Park, Limerick

Māori All Blacks 14
(James Lowe, Ambrose Curtis tries; Otere Black 2 con)

Munster 27
(Niall Scannell, Darren Sweetnam, Ronan O'Mahony tries, penalty try; Ian Keatley 2 con, pen)

Māori All Blacks

15 Marty McKenzie
14 Ambrose Curtis
13 Matt Proctor
12 Tim Bateman
11 James Lowe
10 Otere Black
9 Billy Guyton
8 Akira Ioane
7 Shane Christie
6 Reed Prinsep
5 Jacob Skeen
4 Leighton Price
3 Ben May
2 Ash Dixon (c)
1 Kane Hames

Reserves
16 Leni Apisai
17 Chris Eves
18 Marcel Renata
19 Whetukamokamo Douglas
20 Kara Pryor
21 Brad Weber
22 Ihaia West
23 Jason Emery

Munster

15 Andrew Conway
14 Darren Sweetnam
13 Jaco Taute
12 Rory Scannell
11 Ronan O'Mahony
10 Ian Keatley
9 Duncan Williams
8 Robin Copeland
7 Conor Oliver
6 Tommy O'Donnell (c)
5 Darren O'Shea
4 John Madigan
3 Stephen Archer
2 Niall Scannell
1 James Cronin

Reserves
16 Rhys Marshall
17 Peter McCabe
18 Brian Scott
19 Seán O'Connor
20 John Foley
21 Te Aihe Toma
22 Dan Goggin
23 Alex Wootton

Tommy O'Donnell of Munster leads his team out. STEPHEN POND/GETTY IMAGES

'We got a message through to the Munster management before the match with an explanation of our haka "Te Tīmatanga" and what it meant. At the end it said that we believed Axel Foley was the personification of our haka and we would like to devote this haka to him . . .'

— LUKE CRAWFORD, MĀORI ALL BLACKS KAUMĀTUA

IRISH RUGBY WAS TORN between celebrating and hurting when the Māori All Blacks encountered Munster on a bitterly cold Limerick night in 2016. While their national side had just beaten the All Blacks for the first time in 111 years of trying, they had also just lost one of their favourite sons.

Born and bred in Limerick, Anthony 'Axel' Foley was a legend of Irish rugby with over 200 appearances for Munster and more than 60 for Ireland. He joined Munster's coaching staff after retiring as a player in 2008 and became head coach in 2014. An uncompromising player, talismanic leader and inspirational coach, Foley defined Munster rugby on and off the field. On 16 October 2016, Foley passed away in his sleep while staying with the Munster squad in Paris. He was just 42 years old and was survived by two young sons.

> *Kua hinga he tōtara haemata i te wao nui a Tāne*
> *A lofty tōtara tree has fallen in the great forest of Tāne*

Foley's passing was felt hard not only in Ireland but also across the global rugby community where he was considered to be someone who embodied the values, traditions and spirit of rugby.

Two weeks after his passing, the All Blacks met Ireland in a clash at Chicago's famed NFL stadium Soldier Field. Led by Munster players CJ Stander, Simon Zebo, Conor Murray and Donnacha Ryan, Ireland faced up to the haka in the shape of the number 8 to pay tribute to Foley and the jersey he so proudly wore for both Ireland and Munster. It was an emotional tribute from Ireland and one that helped spur the side on to their first-ever victory over the All Blacks by a margin of 40–29. In a statement released after the match, Foley's family said how much the display meant to them:

> To say that we were touched by how Ireland faced the New Zealand haka, drawing inspiration from the No. 8, would be an understatement. Ironically, 15 years ago, Anthony played for Ireland against New Zealand and lost on a score of 40–29. Last night's Irish response to the haka was an incredible remembrance.

The following week it was the Māori All Blacks looking to pay tribute to Foley when they faced Munster in Limerick. While Foley's passing loomed large over the build-up to the match, so too did Munster's rich history with New Zealand.

In 1978, Munster became the first Irish side to beat the All Blacks when they claimed a 12–0

victory to deny the All Blacks an unbeaten northern hemisphere tour. Three decades later, it took a last-gasp Joe Rokocoko try to snatch a nail-biting 18–16 win for the All Blacks in the 30-year anniversary of the classic 1978 match. It was an occasion that also included not one, but two, memorable haka. Prior to the All Blacks haka, New Zealand players Rua Tipoki, Doug Howlett, Lifeimi Mafi and Jerry Manning stirred the home crowd into a frenzy by stepping out of the Munster line to perform 'Ka Mate'. Former Māori All Blacks captain Tipoki told *Stuff* that the opportunity to challenge the All Blacks with a haka was the next best thing to performing it for them:

> It was a once in a lifetime opportunity. We got asked to represent our team. We weren't sure but we spoke to everyone and that's what they wanted us to do on behalf of our team. So it was a special moment in my career and I will always remember it.

While Munster's New Zealand quartet performed their haka to a raucous reaction from the crowd, the All Blacks laid down their challenge to an eerily quiet stadium. The Thomond Park faithful fell silent in the ultimate show of respect as captain Piri Weepu led the All Blacks' response. 'It was a challenge for me to step up and challenge them back and I think the boys stepped up to that tonight. We met the challenge,' Weepu said.

Munster's rivalry with New Zealand rugby ran deep and a first-ever victory over the Māori All Blacks would no doubt add to the legacy. With so much history and emotion bubbling to the surface in the days leading up to the match, Māori All Blacks kaumātua [elder] Luke Crawford explains that the entire squad was united in showing their respect for Anthony Foley:

> Māori tikanga [custom] is at the core of how our team operates and our tikanga demanded we pay respect to Axel. We

Opposite A view from the stands of 'Te Tīmatanga' being performed. DIARMUID GREENE/SPORTSFILE VIA GETTY IMAGES

were well aware of his legendary status and effigies of him loomed large all over Limerick. We could see that, to his people, Axel had moved beyond legend status to another level that in our world he would be classified as a tipua [supernatural] so how do we show the appropriate respect to someone of such status?

The boys responded that they wanted to do something personal. We held wānanga [deep discussions] over the course of the week and collectively agreed to takoha [gift] a jersey and to perform our haka over the top of the jersey to imbue our aroha [respect] to Axel, his whānau [family] and the Munster team. We were sure that the gesture was the right thing to do because in Māori custom it was tika [correct].

We got a message through to the Munster management before the match with an explanation of our haka 'Te Tīmatanga' and what it meant. At the end it said that we believed Axel Foley was the personification of our haka and we would like to devote this haka to him and present your team with a jersey.

On cue, the rain began to pelt down as the Māori All Blacks lined up to perform the haka in front of a packed Thomond Park. The Munster side stood shoulder to shoulder, attempting to contain the emotion of the occasion as Māori All Blacks captain Ash Dixon walked through the middle of the haka formation. Flanked by senior teammates Joe Royal, Matt Proctor and Tim Bateman, Dixon stopped on the halfway line, staring intently at the Munster team.

With the crowd of 25,000 in complete silence, Dixon unfurled a Māori All Blacks jersey with the initials AF inscribed on the back and placed it gently on the halfway line, all the while not taking his eyes off the Munster team. Seconds later, rapturous applause reverberated around the stands as the crowd realised the significance of the gift. The four players then marched backwards to rejoin their teammates as the ovation grew louder.

Without missing a beat, Dixon slotted into the formation to lead the Māori All Blacks in a touching performance of 'Te Tīmatanga' in the driving rain. In a seldom-seen gesture, the Māori All Blacks management performed the haka on the sideline at the same time. It was a fitting tribute to the life of Anthony Foley, and a performance that will live long in the memories of those who were there to experience it.

Luke Crawford picks up the story at a moment that nearly brought both teams to tears:

> Then Axel's two young boys were led on to the field to collect the jersey from Ash. Our boys were all emotional and Munster almost broke too. Their captain said to us after, 'We meant no disrespect by breaking away early during the presentation of the jersey, but we were extremely emotional and before such a big battle there was no place for tears. We couldn't have that, so we broke away to regroup, it was too emotional.'

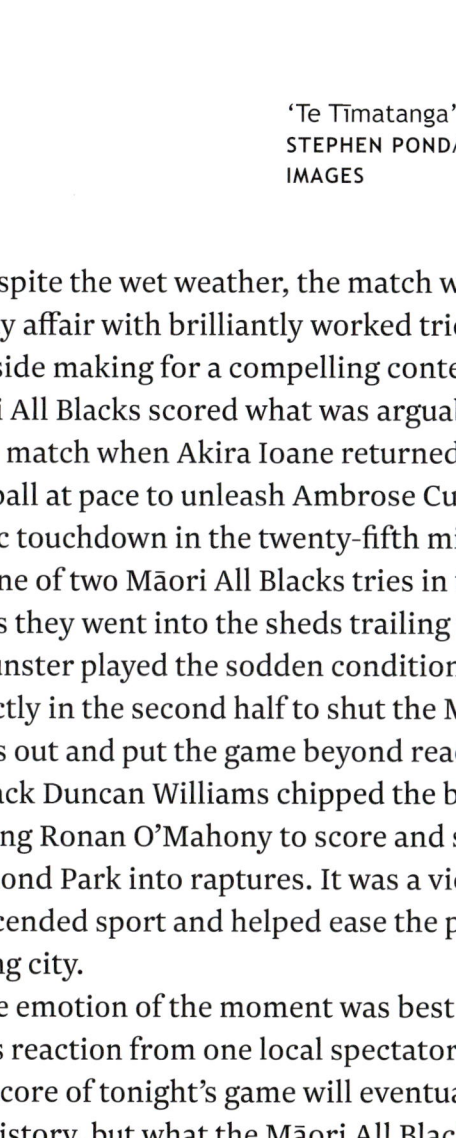

'Te Tīmatanga' in action.
STEPHEN POND/GETTY IMAGES

Despite the wet weather, the match was a high-quality affair with brilliantly worked tries from each side making for a compelling contest. The Māori All Blacks scored what was arguably the try of the match when Akira Ioane returned a soaring high ball at pace to unleash Ambrose Curtis for a classic touchdown in the twenty-fifth minute. It was one of two Māori All Blacks tries in the first half as they went into the sheds trailing 17–14.

Munster played the sodden conditions perfectly in the second half to shut the Māori All Blacks out and put the game beyond reach when halfback Duncan Williams chipped the ball over for wing Ronan O'Mahony to score and send Thomond Park into raptures. It was a victory that transcended sport and helped ease the pain for a hurting city.

The emotion of the moment was best captured in this reaction from one local spectator: 'The final score of tonight's game will eventually fade into history, but what the Māori All Blacks have done here tonight will remain in our memory for all time.'

TE TĪMATANGA FOR AN IRISH ICON / 233

Below Darren Sweetnam of Munster celebrates after scoring his side's third try of the match. BRENDAN MORAN/SPORTSFILE VIA GETTY IMAGES

Opposite top Ronan O'Mahony, the fourth try-scorer for Munster, is congratulated by teammates Robin Copeland (left) and Jaco Taute. DIARMUID GREENE/SPORTSFILE VIA GETTY IMAGES

Opposite below The scoreboard tells the story. STEPHEN POND/GETTY IMAGES

TE TĪMATANGA FOR AN IRISH ICON / 235

PASIFIKA POWER

Opposite Byron Kelleher is thrown in a tackle. **PHIL WALTER/GETTY IMAGES**

10 July 2004
North Harbour Stadium, Albany

All Blacks 41
(Joe Rokocoko 2, Rico Gear, Justin Marshall, Kees Meeuws, Tana Umaga tries; Dan Carter 4 con, pen)

Pacific Islanders 26
(Sitiveni Sivivatu 2, Seru Rabini, Sione Lauaki tries; Seremaia Baikeinuku 3 con)

All Blacks

15 Mils Muliaina
14 Rico Gear
13 Tana Umaga (c)
12 Dan Carter
11 Joe Rokocoko
10 Carlos Spencer
9 Justin Marshall
8 Xavier Rush
7 Marty Holah
6 Jono Gibbes
5 Keith Robinson
4 Chris Jack
3 Carl Hayman
2 Keven Mealamu
1 Kees Meeuws

Reserves

16 Andrew Hore
17 Greg Somerville
18 Jerry Collins
19 Mose Tuiali'i
20 Byron Kelleher
21 Nick Evans
22 Sam Tuitupou

Pacific Islanders

15 Seru Rabeni
14 Lome Fa'atau
13 Brian Lima
12 Seremaia Baikeinuku
11 Sitiveni Sivivatu
10 Tanner Vili
9 Moses Rauluni
8 Sisa Koyamaibole
7 Alifereti Doviverata
6 Sione Lauaki
5 Ifereimi Rawaqa
4 Inoke Afeaki (c)
3 Taufa'ao Filise
2 Aleki Lutui
1 Soane Tonga'uiha

Reserves

16 Joeli Lotawa
17 Tevita Taumoepeau
18 Filipo Levi
19 Semo Sititi
20 Steve So'oialo
21 Tane Tu'ipulotu
22 Sireli Bobo

Opposite top The Pacific Islanders challenge the All Blacks, performing a hybrid version of the Fijian Cibi, the Tongan Sipi Tau and the Sāmoan Siva Tau. MICHAEL BRADLEY/GETTY IMAGES

Opposite below The All Blacks respond to the challenge laid down by the Pacific Islanders. MICHAEL BRADLEY/GETTY IMAGES

'We throw everything in, including the kitchen sink, and strive for excellence along the way. Big hits are the culture here in New Zealand. As long as they're legal and fair, the All Blacks boys will welcome it.'
— INOKE AFEAKI, PACIFIC ISLANDERS CAPTAIN

OH, WHAT MIGHT HAVE been. Red, white and blue are the colours of many a professional sports team, but for a brief period in the early 2000s those colours featured on the jersey of a rugby side that had been a long time in the making. The red was for Tonga, the white for Fiji and the blue for Sāmoa.

In 2004, the combined Pacific Islanders side made its way on to the international stage, as a way of pooling the collectively undeniable talent of the three nations. The Pacific Islanders came in, performed creditably against almost all of their top-tier opposition, then disappeared only a few years later.

Ever since, there have been calls for the re-formation of the side to compete in Super Rugby, or even test level again, as a South Pacific alternative to the British & Irish Lions. But for now, all we have are memories of a team that played wildly entertaining rugby, including an incredibly fun test against the All Blacks not long after its inception.

In the 2004 season, New Zealanders were still coming to grips with the fact that the All Blacks had failed at yet another World Cup the year before. The semi-final loss to the Wallabies at the tournament had cost coach John Mitchell his job, and Reuben Thorne his place as captain.

New coach Graham Henry had come in and immediately made one change that would be of long-term benefit to the team, placing Dan Carter in his starting XV. As well as that new-dawn story, there was also a bit of a fairy-tale ending to another one. Xavier Rush looked to have been destined to be a one-test All Black after he'd been picked by a desperate John Hart for the third 1998 Bledisloe Cup test, then discarded after the test ended with the All Blacks' fifth defeat of the season. But six seasons of hard graft with the Blues and Auckland saw Henry give the now 27-year-old another shot at the big time. The All Blacks had already had three test matches that season, whipping the newly crowned world champion English in two tests and then easily dispatching Argentina in another.

While the All Blacks were still heavily favoured to win the first-ever test match between the two sides, there were plenty of familiar names in the Pacific Islanders side. Tongan hooker Aleki Lutui had been exciting crowds with his expansive range of skills for Bay of Plenty and the Chiefs. Sione Lauaki had enjoyed a breakout year in Super Rugby for the Chiefs as well, scoring a memorable solo try on Eden Park to win a game against the Blues. Veteran Sāmoan back Brian Lima was still capable of delivering tackles that led to him being

Opposite top Halfback Justin Marshall can only watch as Sione Lauaki runs away to score. **PHOTOSPORT**

Opposite below A gap is created as Keven Mealamu bursts through a tackle from the Pacific Islanders. **PHOTOSPORT**

dubbed 'The Chiropractor'. Fijian-born winger Sitiveni Sivivatu was pegged as one to watch, while on the bench Filipo Levi was a provincial stalwart for Otago.

The teams hit the field on North Harbour Stadium on a cool July night, and the anticipation built for the challenge to the haka. The Pacific Islanders merged the three countries' traditional challenges—the Fijian Cibi, the Tongan Sipi Tau and the Sāmoan Siva Tau—into one, and also had another unique addition up their sleeves. The hybrid version was not led by a player, but rather by trainer Dominic Fonoti, who was dressed in a traditional Sāmoan lavalava. The All Blacks responded with 'Ka Mate', and the test was ready to get under way in front of 22,000 people.

This wasn't the first time the Pacific Islanders had played an official match, though. They'd recently completed a short tour of Australia, where they'd beaten a Queensland XV and New South Wales before losing to the Wallabies 29–14. However, the test got off to a nightmare start for them when a Carlos Spencer kick took a miraculous bounce to end up in Joe Rokocoko's arms for a try after only a minute of play.

But the men from the Pacific didn't lie down. They took the game straight back to the All Blacks and dominated possession and territory for the next five minutes. Prop Taufa'ao Filise went on a one-man rampage to within five metres of the line, then Seremaia Baikeinuku flicked a pass off his fingertips to fullback Seru Rabeni. The Fijian stepped inside the clutches of Kees Meeuws and Justin Marshall to dot down under the bar, which Baikeinuku converted to put the Pacific Islanders in front. Once again, as when Sāmoa had played their first test at Eden Park back in 1993, there was a huge contingent of Pacific Island fans who were making their voices heard loud and clear.

They'd get even louder. After Marshall had scored another unconverted try, Lauaki set off on a run down the left wing, showing significant pace for a man his size. He passed inside to Sivivatu, who scored under the posts and incredibly gave the visitors the lead again. The fact that the try was a creation of those two players definitely left an impression on Henry, who would have been more than concerned at the scoreline. The All Blacks were stung into action and responded with tries to Rico Gear and Kees Meeuws, to give them a 27–14 lead at the break. But the Pacific Islanders weren't about to roll over and die, with the try of the match coming from a chip ahead by Fijian lock Ifereimi Rawaqa for Sivivatu to score his second.

Then, a bit of comedy as referee Stuart Dickinson of Australia missed a massive bit of cheating at a ruck on halfway, when Inoke Afeaki blatantly raked the ball away while it was on the All Blacks' side. It rolled forward anyway to a very offside Lauaki, who picked it up, looked at Dickinson very guiltily, then jogged away. Once it became clear that the referee had no intention of stopping play, Lauaki swatted off a tackle from Marshall and ran the remaining 40 metres to score. It was now 34–26 and the All Blacks were in a far tougher test match than perhaps anticipated.

There was no fairy-tale comeback for the Pacific Islanders, though, as the All Blacks reverted to

The Pacific Islanders face the haka. PHOTOSPORT

type and closed out the remaining 20 minutes, with Tana Umaga (the first Pasifika man to captain the All Blacks) scoring on full-time to finish the game. In all, though, a commendable result for the combination Pacific Island team. Dreams of this becoming a regular fixture, and the start of something special, were already formulating in the heads of those in attendance and around New Zealand.

But the 2004 test was the one and only time the All Blacks ever played the Pacific Islanders. Fiji, Tonga and Manu Sāmoa all had their own priorities to look after—namely qualifying for the World Cup. Besides, once again the All Blacks had treated the test as a virtual trial and eventually picked the stars Sivivatu and Lauaki to represent New Zealand instead. It meant that the side formed again two years later but only played against northern hemisphere sides, then again in 2008. By 2009, the Sāmoa Rugby Union had decided that the venture wasn't financially viable and pulled out, ending the short lifespan of the Pacific Islanders. Since then, there have been calls for the concept to be revived and compete in Super Rugby, even using Auckland as a home venue. So far, though, it remains a suggestion rather than a reality.

PASIFIKA POWER / 245

FROM LEADING THE HAKA TO FACING IT

Opposite The All Blacks perform the haka in front of an England side that includes Kiwi Riki Flutey.
RICHARD HEATHCOTE/GETTY IMAGES

29 November 2008
Twickenham, London

All Blacks 32
(Mils Muliaina 2, Ma'a Nonu tries;
Dan Carter 5 pen, con)

England 6
(Delon Armitage pen, Toby Flood pen)

All Blacks	**England**
15 Mils Muliaina	15 Delon Armitage
14 Joe Rokocoko	14 Paul Sackey
13 Conrad Smith	13 Jamie Noon
12 Ma'a Nonu	12 Riki Flutey
11 Sitiveni Sivivatu	11 Ugo Monye
10 Dan Carter	10 Toby Flood
9 Jimmy Cowan	9 Danny Care
8 Rodney So'oialo	8 Nick Easter
7 Richie McCaw (c)	7 Michael Lipman
6 Jerome Kaino	6 James Haskell
5 Ali Williams	5 Nick Kennedy
4 Brad Thorn	4 Steve Borthwick (c)
3 Neemia Tialata	3 Phil Vickery
2 Keven Mealamu	2 Lee Mears
1 Tony Woodcock	1 Tim Payne

Reserves

16 Hika Elliot	16 Dylan Hartley
17 John Afoa	17 Matt Stevens
18 Anthony Boric	18 Tom Croft
19 Kieran Read	19 Tom Rees
20 Piri Weepu	20 Harry Ellis
21 Stephen Donald	21 Danny Cipriani
22 Isaia Toeava	22 Dan Hipkiss

Riki Flutey (just right of the ground camera) and his England teammates face the haka. GARETH FULLER/ PA IMAGES VIA GETTY IMAGES

'People were asking me what the best approach was to facing the haka. I said, "Just stand there, stare them in the eye, respect the haka, then go and get on with the game."'

—RIKI FLUTEY, NEW ZEALAND MĀORI, ENGLAND AND BRITISH & IRISH LIONS TEST PLAYER

WHEN WAIRARAPA-BORN RIKI FLUTEY led the haka for the New Zealand Under-19s at the World Championship in 1999, he probably never thought he would end up on the opposing side of an All Blacks haka one day. But that's exactly what happened when the former Māori All Blacks, Te Aute College and Wellington Hurricanes star ran out for England against the All Blacks in November 2008.

While there are several players who have performed the haka for New Zealand age-grade sides before facing it when representing other national unions, Flutey's story is even more noteworthy given his strong ties to Māori culture and tikanga, in which he was immersed throughout his upbringing and while attending the prestigious Māori boarding school Te Aute College in Hawke's Bay.

Steeped in history and guided by Māoritanga principles, Te Aute College has a proud record of producing high-performing graduates and instilling in its students a deep understanding of what it means to be Māori. With a storied stable of notable alumni casting their glow over the hallways and sporting fields, students develop a profound respect for Māori culture, traditions and way of life. It was at Te Aute that Flutey's undoubted rugby potential began to really shine.

An immensely talented playmaker and astute tactician, Flutey's silky ball skills and game-breaking ability caught the attention of national selectors. He was chosen for the New Zealand Under-16s in 1996 before spending two years in the New Zealand Secondary Schools, including captaining the side in 1998. Speaking to JP Tocker on the All Blacks podcast, Flutey revealed one of the secrets to his success while at Te Aute:

> I would play First XV for Te Aute College then drive into town to play for Clive on the same day. I would make it there for the second half of the Clive match and play with the men. That taught me a lot—I was only 16 or 17. It toughened me up. When I went back to First XV rugby it seemed a lot easier.

Flutey's rise through the age-group system continued when he joined the Wellington academy in 1999. He was a pivotal member, and haka leader, of the New Zealand Under-19 team that defeated Wales 25–0 in the final of the World Championship that year. It seemed as though destiny was calling Flutey towards a place in the All Blacks. 'It was a dream of mine, just like any other kid in New Zealand, to be an All Black,' he said.

Neemia Tialata (centre) and the All Blacks challenge the English. TONY MARSHALL/PA IMAGES VIA GETTY IMAGES

Able to cover any position in the backline, Flutey's All Blacks dream stalled due to his own versatility, however. Pigeon-holed as a utility player or perfect bench option, Flutey struggled to nail down a regular starting position for the Hurricanes. His talent and ability were undoubted, but coaches didn't seem to know where to use him best. After just five Super Rugby appearances in 2005, he signed with London Irish at the age of 25. 'Back in New Zealand, I wasn't sure whether I was playing at 9, 10, 12 or 15, so I came over here with a clean slate knowing I had to prove I had the goods to start in any of those positions,' Flutey told the *Daily Mail*.

It didn't take long for Flutey to establish himself as one of the most dangerous and creative ball-runners in the English Premiership. Playing at second five-eighth, Flutey perfected the role of a dual playmaker a decade before Beauden Barrett and Richie Mo'unga made it *en vogue* for the All Blacks.

Drums were beating for a call-up to the England squad once Flutey became eligible in September 2008, and England coach Martin Johnson wasted no time selecting him for a packed end-of-year calendar that featured tests against Australia, South Africa and finally the All Blacks at Twickenham. 'There was a lot of media hype around it, me being the Kiwi guy in the England team and playing against the All Blacks,' said Flutey.

In the week leading up to the All Blacks clash, Flutey grew accustomed to answering questions

15
O2
O2

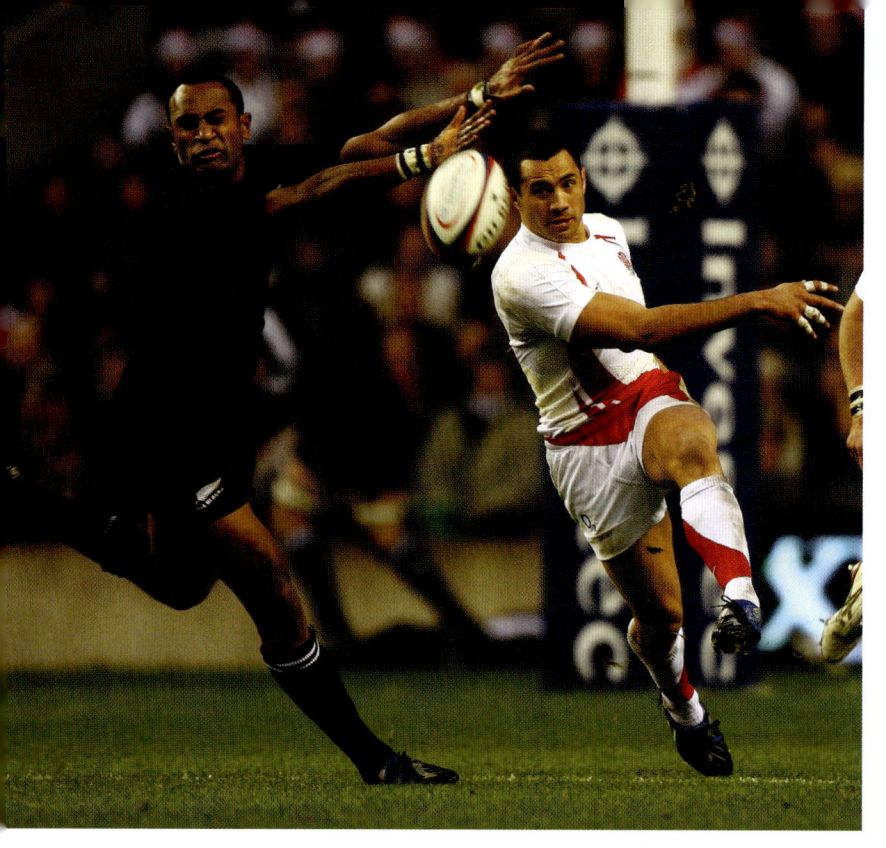

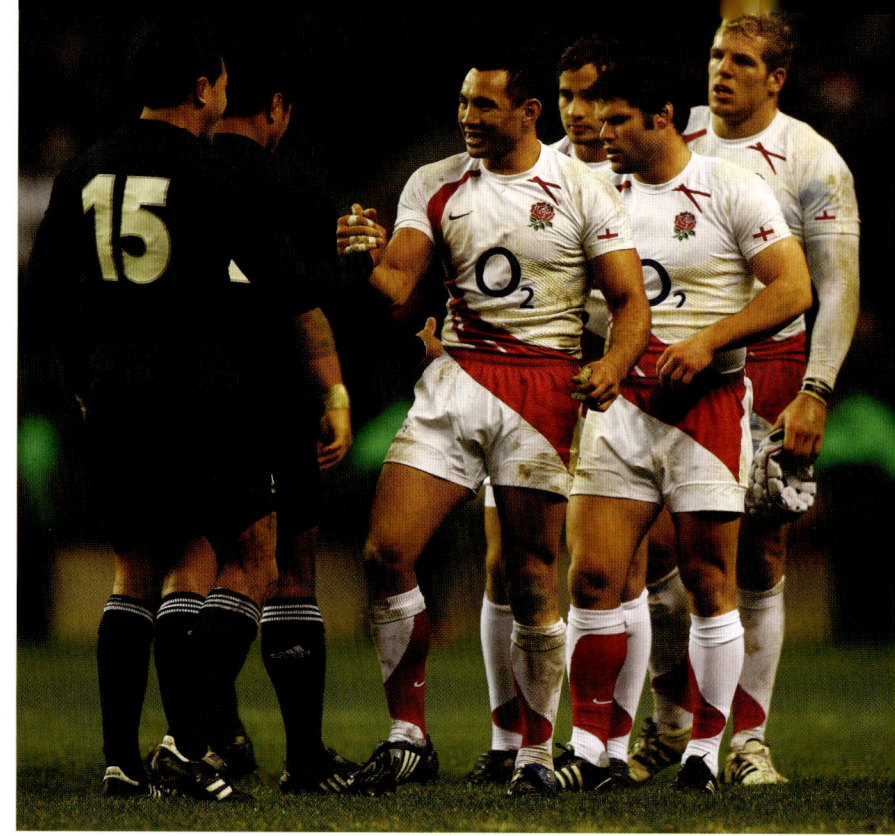

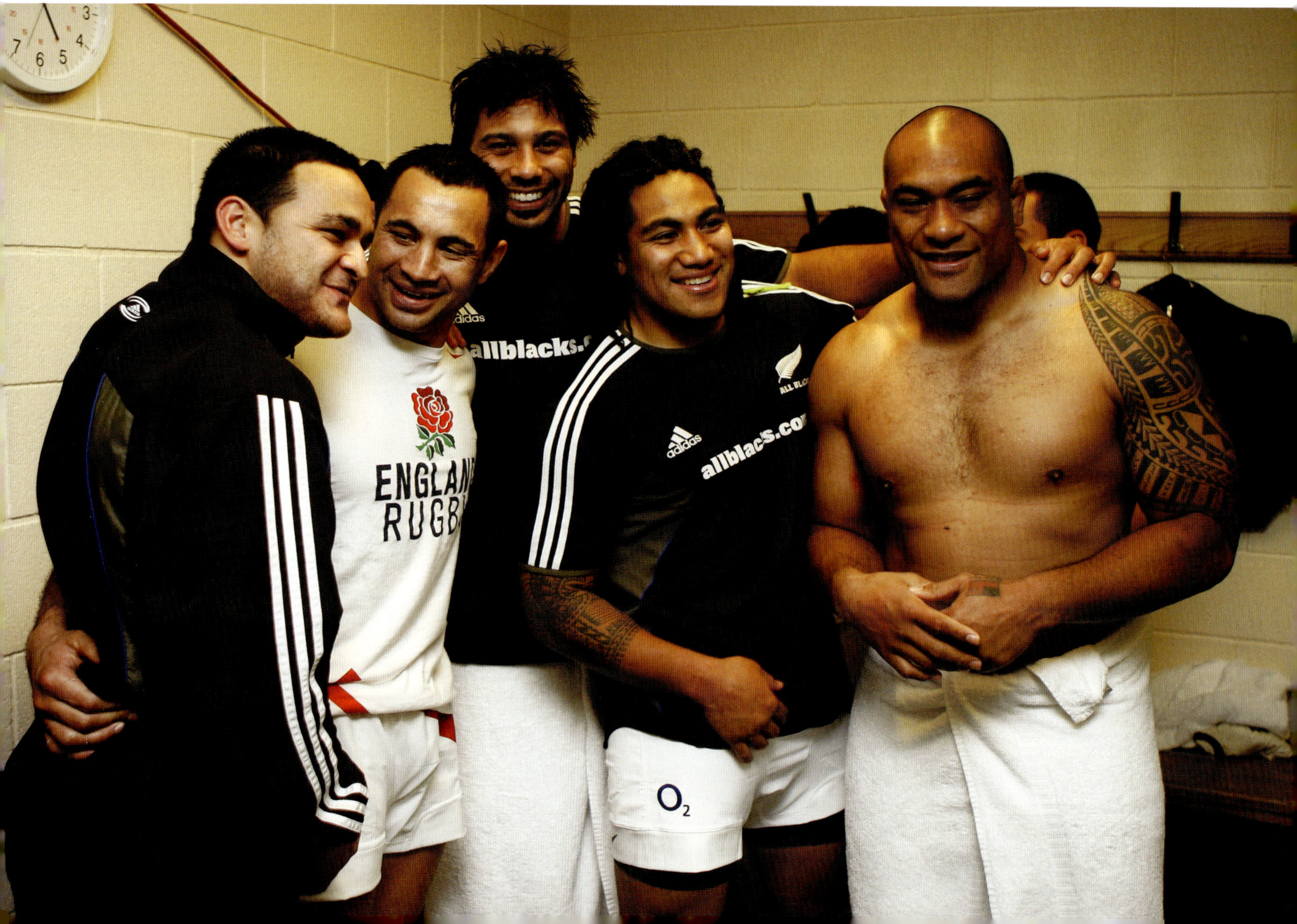
adidas
allblacks.c
ENGLAN
RUGB
adidas
allblacks.co
O2

Opposite top left Riki Flutey kicks under pressure from Joe Rokocoko. RICHARD HEATHCOTE/GETTY IMAGES

Opposite top right Respect. RICHARD HEATHCOTE/GETTY IMAGES

Opposite below All smiles: Flutey and his former Wellington teammates in the changing rooms after the match. ROSS LAND/GETTY IMAGES

about what it would mean to face the haka as a New Zealand-born Māori:

> I spoke to family members and they were right behind me. I also had lunch with Norm Hewitt, the All Blacks hooker, who gave me his blessing which was very important. He went to the same college as me and is someone I really look up to because he's a Māori All Black and a top leader. His words made me want to grab this opportunity.

Flutey lined up in the 12 jersey for England against the All Blacks. He was marking former Hurricanes partner Ma'a Nonu and many of his former teammates from the New Zealand Under-16, New Zealand Secondary Schools and New Zealand Under-19 sides. 'Before the game, people were asking me what the best approach was to facing the haka. I said, "Just stand there, stare them in the eye, respect the haka, then go and get on with the game."'

With 75,000 English fans belting out 'Swing Low, Sweet Chariot', Flutey lined up to face the All Blacks haka. Across from him, another Te Aute College old boy, Piri Weepu, stepped up to lead the All Blacks in their performance of 'Ka Mate'. 'For me . . . I taught a lot of these guys how to do the haka back in New Zealand Under-16 and Under-19 days, when I was the haka leader. I was watching some of them thinking, *Sheesh, come on fellas, that's not how I taught you!*' Flutey's England teammates did exactly as he had recommended during the haka. They linked arms, soaked in the experience, and paid total respect to the challenge.

While the moment will live long in Flutey's memory, the performance of England that day wasn't as notable. England were ragged and ill-disciplined in the face of a rampant All Blacks side and forced to play half the game with 14 men after four players were yellow carded during the match. All Blacks first five-eighth Dan Carter punished England with five penalties, and a brace of tries to Mils Muliaina and another by Ma'a Nonu powered the All Blacks to a completely dominant 32–6 victory.

For Flutey, it would be the only time he would play the All Blacks across his 14 tests for England. The highlight of his international career was yet to come, though. In 2009, Flutey played a key role in the British & Irish Lions third-test victory over South Africa and in the process became the first man in history to play both for and against the Lions, an honour he's particularly proud of.

'To get the opportunity to play at the highest level and to play against the best players in the world was massive for me. And to kick on from that and to represent the Lions on the 2009 tour of South Africa was a massive highlight of my career.'

THE WELSH STALEMATE

Opposite The dressing-room haka. ROSS LAND/AFP VIA GETTY IMAGES

**25 November 2006
Millennium Stadium, Cardiff**

All Blacks 45
(Sitiveni Sivivatu 3, Luke McAlister tries, penalty try; Dan Carter 4 pen, 2 con, Nick Evans 2 con)

Wales 10
(Martyn Williams try; James Hook con, Stephen Jones pen)

All Blacks		**Wales**	
15	Mils Muliaina	15	Kevin Morgan
14	Rico Gear	14	Mark Jones
13	Conrad Smith	13	Tom Shanklin
12	Luke McAlister	12	Sonny Parker
11	Sitiveni Sivivatu	11	Shane Williams
10	Dan Carter	10	Stephen Jones (c)
9	Byron Kelleher	9	Dwayne Peel
8	Rodney So'oialo	8	Ryan Jones
7	Richie McCaw (c)	7	Martyn Williams
6	Jerry Collins	6	Jonathan Thomas
5	Ali Williams	5	Ian Evans
4	Keith Robinson	4	Ian Gough
3	Carl Hayman	3	Adam Jones
2	Anton Oliver	2	T. Rhys Thomas
1	Neemia Tialata	1	Duncan Jones

Reserves		**Reserves**	
16	Andrew Hore	16	Matthew Rees
17	Tony Woodcock	17	Gethin Jenkins
18	James Ryan	18	Alun Wyn Jones
19	Reuben Thorne	19	Alix Popham
20	Piri Weepu	20	Mike Phillips
21	Nick Evans	21	James Hook
22	Ma'a Nonu	22	Gavin Henson

The All Blacks practise the haka during a training session at Millennium Stadium in Cardiff. DAVID DAVIES/PA IMAGES VIA GETTY IMAGES

'If the other team wants to mess around, we'll just do the haka in the shed. At the end of the day, haka is about spiritual preparation and we do it for ourselves.'
—RICHIE MCCAW, ALL BLACKS CAPTAIN

ONE OF THE MORE infamous moments in haka history occurred in 2006 when the All Blacks performed 'Ka Mate' in their changing room instead of in the middle of Cardiff's Millennium Stadium.

As the pre-recorded haka played silently on the giant screens at the national stadium of Wales, the gasps and groans of over 70,000 Welsh fans grew louder, recognising that they had been robbed of witnessing one of rugby's most cherished traditions in the flesh. The decision to perform the haka in the changing sheds was not taken lightly by the All Blacks and stemmed back to their clash the year before.

That 2005 centenary test marked 100 years since the All Blacks and Wales had first met, a game where Wales defeated the All Blacks 3–0 at Cardiff Arms Park (the site where Millennium Stadium would eventually be built). To mark the occasion, the All Blacks agreed to move the timing of the haka from its normal position before kick-off to in between the national anthems. This aligned with the order of events in 1905 and served to pay homage to the Wales side that handed the 'Originals' the only loss of their 35-match, five-month-long tour of the British Isles, France and USA.

Although agreed to as a one-off gesture as part of the centenary celebrations, the Welsh Rugby Union requested that the All Blacks perform the haka in between the anthems once again in 2006. The request was swiftly rejected and a stalemate was reached, with captain Richie McCaw saying after the game that his side was left with no choice but to perform the haka in the changing room:

> It's disappointing for fans but it's been traditional to do it the way it's been done and there wasn't a good reason to change it. If the other team wants to mess around, we'll just do the haka in the shed. At the end of the day, haka is about spiritual preparation and we do it for ourselves.

A lone camera was snuck in to the All Blacks' changing room to capture the haka. Recorded from an up-close and awkward angle, the All Blacks huddled tightly together, staring intently forward at an invisible foe. Wing Rico Gear navigated between the hulking bodies before piercing the silence with a thunderous war cry:

Ringa pākia!

With that, the All Blacks came together as one. There was to be no phoning in this performance despite the sterile surroundings.

Opposite top Sitiveni Sivivatu breaks free from the tackle of Wales' Stephen Jones on his way to the tryline. PAUL ELLIS/ AFP VIA GETTY IMAGES

Opposite below The stand-off in 2008: Wales don't want to budge despite referee Jonathan Kaplan's insistence. STU FORSTER/ GETTY IMAGES

The decibels climbed several notches when the other 21 All Blacks joined in with their kaea. The slapping of thighs and the banging of hands on chests reverberated around the bare changing room as the All Blacks advanced towards a blank wall in a crescendo of hype and passion:

A upane kaupane whiti te rā!
Hī!

And then silence. There was to be none of the usual rapturous applause from thousands of spectators. Instead, the All Blacks turned and marched towards the door in near quiet. This was one haka that fans would not watch live, but only on pre-recorded tape minutes later.

Despite not beating the All Blacks since 1953, Wales came into the test with an expectation of pushing the All Blacks close at the same ground (although redeveloped several times since) where they had secured their three previous victories against the men in black. But any thoughts of a long-awaited triumph were soon extinguished as the All Blacks' powerful front row of Neemia Tialata, Anton Oliver and Carl Hayman savagely twisted the Welsh pack in the first scrum of the game. It was a massive psychological blow for the Welsh side, who expected to muscle up to the All Blacks upfront and stretch them out wide. In the end, they could do neither as the All Blacks dominated virtually every facet of the game to win 45–10 with flying wing Sitiveni Sivivatu crossing for a hat-trick of tries.

TWO YEARS LATER, THE teams met again at Millennium Stadium with more drama surrounding the haka. This time there was no controversy around its timing—instead it was the minute following the challenge that turned heads around the world.

Once the All Blacks' haka was completed, the Welsh team stood their ground on the 40-metre mark, unmoving and staring straight into the eyes of their fired-up opponents. Like a scene from a western movie, the All Blacks refused to budge and enacted a fully-fledged Mexican stand-off with their opponents in red.

Separated by 20 metres of grass in the middle of the stadium, neither team was willing to break the impasse as referee Jonathan Kaplan made his way up and down the All Blacks' line ordering them to get ready for kick-off. Eventually, after 90 long seconds, the All Blacks were the first team to break as they made their way back, knowing that their challenge was well and truly accepted.

After 40 minutes, there was no doubting that the tactic had worked to lift Wales as they went into the sheds with a 9–6 lead on the back of three penalties from first five-eighth Stephen Jones. The lead was short-lived, though, as Dan Carter struck a penalty goal early in the second half and Ma'a Nonu and Jerome Kaino crossed for tries to take control of the match and secure a comfortable 29–9 victory.

WATER

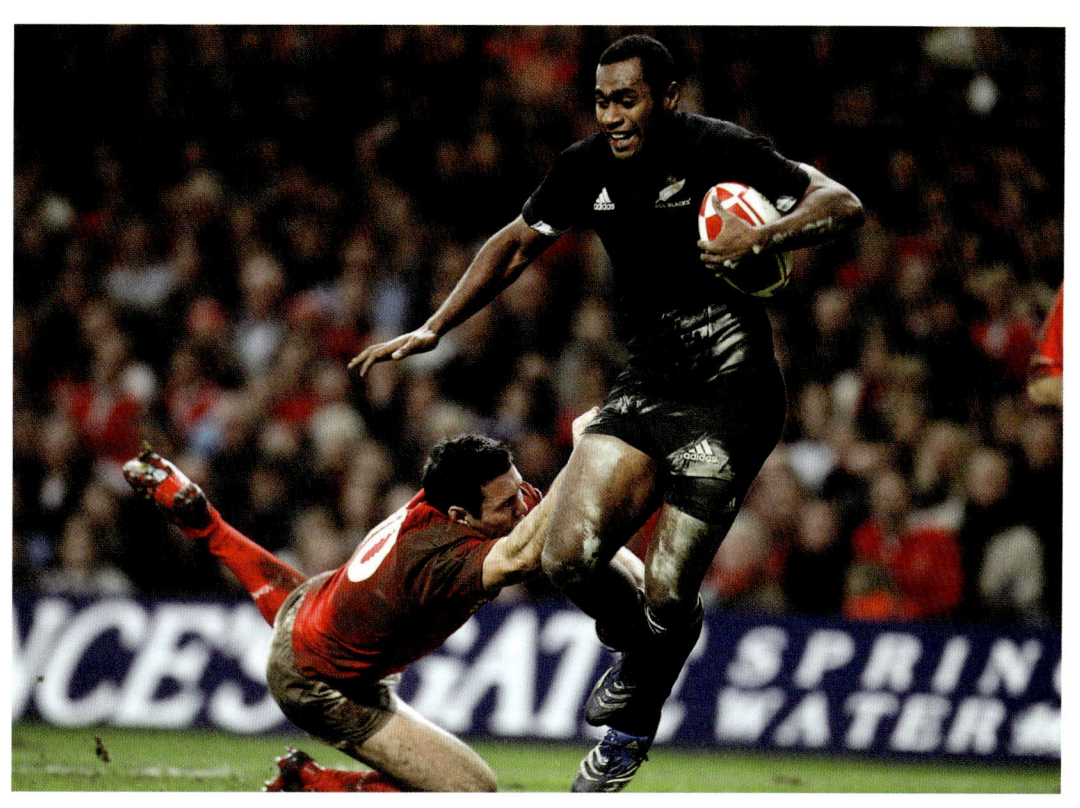

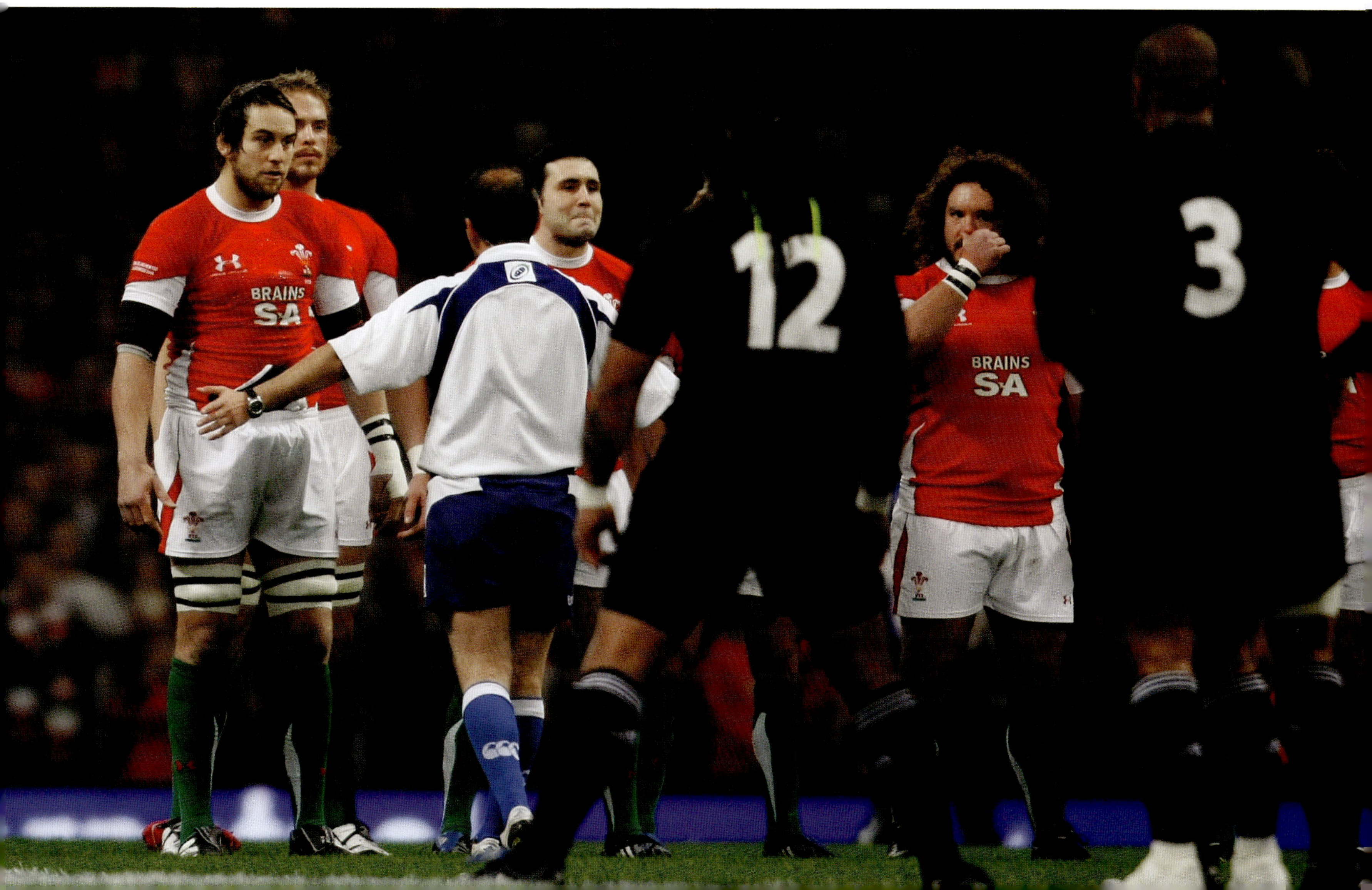
BRAINS
SA
12
3
BRAINS
SA

THE BRAVE BLOSSOMS STARE DOWN THE CHALLENGE

Opposite Luke Whitelock, All Blacks captain for the day, takes his place at the front of the formation.
HANNAH PETERS/GETTY IMAGES

3 November 2018
Ajinomoto Stadium, Tokyo

All Blacks 69
(Ngani Laumape 3, George Bridge 2, Dane Coles, Waisake Naholo, Matt Proctor, Te Toiroa Tahuriorangi, Richie Mo'unga tries; Mo'unga 7 con, pen, Jordie Barrett con)

Japan 31
(Timothy Lafaele 2, Hendrik Tui, Samuela Anise, Jamie Henry tries; Yu Tamara 3 con)

All Blacks
15 Jordie Barrett
14 Nehe Milner-Skudder
13 Matt Proctor
12 Ngani Laumape
11 Waisake Naholo
10 Richie Mo'unga
9 Te Toiroa Tahuriorangi
8 Luke Whitelock (c)
7 Dalton Papali'i
6 Vaea Fifita
5 Jackson Hemopo
4 Patrick Tuipulotu
3 Angus Ta'avao
2 Dane Coles
1 Ofa Tuungafasi

Reserves
16 Liam Coltman
17 Tim Perry
18 Tyrel Lomax
19 Dillon Hunt
20 Gareth Evans
21 Mitchell Drummond
22 Brett Cameron
23 George Bridge

Japan
15 Ryohei Yamanaka
14 Jamie Henry
13 Will Tupou
12 Timothy Lafaele
11 Kenki Fukuoka
10 Yu Tamura
9 Yutaka Nagare
8 Hendrik Tui
7 Kazuki Himeno
6 Michael Leitch (c)
5 Samuela Anisi
4 Wimpie van der Walt
3 Hiroshi Yamashita
2 Atsushi Sakate
1 Keita Inagaki

Reserves
16 Yusuke Niwai
17 Masataka Mikami
18 Asaeli Ai Valu
19 Uwe Helu
20 Isileli Nakajima
21 Fumiaki Tanaka
22 Rikiya Matsuda
23 Ryoto Nakamura

Opposite top The Tokyo crowd stayed dead silent for the duration of 'Ka Mate'. KYODO NEWS STILLS VIA GETTY IMAGES

Opposite below Japanese skipper Michael Leitch (or *Rīchi Maikeru* to the locals) spearheads his team's response to the haka. KYODO NEWS STILLS VIA GETTY IMAGES

'I can feel their fighting spirit. When we line up and we are watching the All Blacks perform the haka, it makes me think to myself, *We can do it!*'

—SHOTA HORIE, JAPAN AND FORMER OTAGO HOOKER

BRAVE BLOSSOMS: NOT EXACTLY a name that strikes fear into the hearts of the opposition, right?

With all due respect, fans could have been forgiven for thinking that before the All Blacks faced Japan in November 2018. The name itself isn't actually a quaint translation from Japanese to English as popularly thought, but rather the evolution of the old 'Cherry Blossom' nickname for the team that pertained to its red-and-white hooped jerseys. The 'Brave' was added by Tokyo-based English journalist Rich Freeman in 2003 after the team's impressive (albeit losing) display against Scotland in the World Cup. The Japan Rugby Football Union was apparently not too fond of it at first, yet embraced the moniker once it became clear that it had grown popular with local fans after the side's breakthrough win over the Springboks in 2015.

However, as brave as they were, their 2018 meeting with the All Blacks had the makings of a walk in the park for the then world champions. With their Rugby World Cup defence looming less than a year later, it seemed like more of an opportunity for the All Blacks to familiarise themselves with the conditions in Japan rather than to play a competitive test match. After all, the All Blacks' average winning margin against Japan going into the test was a staggering 83 points.

A quick perusal of social media comments in the week leading up to the test showed that the Brave Blossoms were considered no more than a glorified training run for the All Blacks. *Could the All Blacks challenge their record score of 145 against Japan at the 1995 Rugby World Cup?* some fans mused.

The week before, the All Blacks had dispatched Australia 37–20 at Nissan Stadium to complete a Bledisloe Cup clean sweep for the season. With blockbuster test matches against England, Ireland and Italy to follow in the coming weeks, the All Blacks management decided to send the bulk of the squad on to Europe in advance and field a largely inexperienced side for the Japan clash.

Eight debutants were named in an All Blacks' match-day 23 that bore little resemblance to the one that had thumped Australia just a week earlier. Dane Coles was the most experienced player in the side, owning over a third of its total caps with 56; Waisake Naholo came a distant second with 24. Speaking the day prior to the match, Japan's inspirational captain Michael Leitch eyed an opportunity against the very green All Blacks.

'When you look at the number of test matches collectively in the [New Zealand] team, it is not so much and their test match experience is not so

Opposite top Richie Mo'unga can't catch Japanese winger Jamie Henry as he dives to score in the corner. KOKI NAGAHAMA/GETTY IMAGES

Opposite below Former Highlanders teammates Fumiaki Tanaka and Waisake Naholo share a joke post-match. HANNAH PETERS/GETTY IMAGES

much there,' said the Japan loose forward. 'There is an opportunity to pressure the leadership group. If we are going to take the All Blacks down then it is going to be tomorrow,' he predicted.

Leitch was no stranger to big-match boilovers, having led Japan to their victory over the Springboks. He knew that the only way to beat the All Blacks was to front them head on—and that started with the haka.

An excitable crowd of over 43,000 at Tokyo Stadium hushed as Nehe Milner-Skudder stepped forward to lead the All Blacks haka. Japanese culture is built on respect and you could have heard a pin drop as Milner-Skudder called the All Blacks to action with their traditional haka 'Ka Mate'.

Then something unexpected happened.

Like some of the All Blacks' more fancied opponents before them, the Japanese marched forward in an arrow formation to the halfway line. With Leitch at the point of the arrowhead, they continued to creep forward as the haka hit a crescendo.

> *A upane! A kaupane!*
> *A upane kaupane whiti te rā!*
> *Hī!*

The haka culminated with Japan standing mere metres away from the All Blacks. The challenge had been accepted. This was a very different Japan to the one that had been drubbed by the All Blacks in their three previous test matches in 1995, 2011 and 2013.

'I can feel their fighting spirit. When we line up and we are watching the All Blacks perform the haka, it makes me think to myself, *We can do it!*' said Japanese hooker for the 2019 World Cup and former Otago Mitre 10 Cup player Shota Horie.

The Brave Blossoms believed they could do the unthinkable, and that belief grew stronger when lock Samuela Anise charged down a Jordie Barrett clearing kick to score the opening try after just three minutes. Japan's dream beginning ignited a dazzling test match. After 80 minutes, exactly 100 points had been scored with the All Blacks prevailing 69–31.

Japan had done what very few teams had achieved in the past and put five tries on the All Blacks—in fact, they'd scored more in one match than the Wallabies had managed in four that year. From clever set-piece movements to sweeping back play and slick forward exchanges, Japan kept the ball moving in a masterclass of high-tempo rugby that tested the All Blacks' defence throughout.

Although Japan couldn't repeat their giant-killing efforts of three years earlier against South Africa, they played their part in one of the most breathless and entertaining test matches seen in recent history.

Both teams came together in mutual respect and admiration following the final whistle. Jerseys were exchanged, embraces were shared, and a collective bow to each corner of the stadium drew more rapturous applause from the adoring audience.

The Brave Blossoms hadn't defeated the All Blacks but had captured the imagination of the

In a foreshadowing of what became a custom at the following year's World Cup, both sides bow to the crowd. KOKI NAGAHAMA/ GETTY IMAGES

Japanese public and given the world a taste of what was to come at the Rugby World Cup 12 months later. On that stage they would triumph over Ireland, Scotland, Sāmoa and Russia to secure a historic quarter-final berth, sparking a passion for rugby in Japanese fans that will live on for generations. It's probably no stretch to say that the host's performance in the pool stages was easily the highlight of a tournament that was dominated early by contentious refereeing and judicial decisions.

Although the All Blacks and the Brave Blossoms never met on the field at the 2019 Rugby World Cup, there was another touching haka moment when the All Blacks landed in Kashiwa to begin their preparations for the tournament. Outside their hotel, they were greeted by a group of schoolchildren performing an impressive haka with all the passion and precision you would expect from the All Blacks themselves. According to All Blacks coach Steve Hansen, it was a moment that encapsulated the deep respect which exists between Japanese and New Zealand rugby. 'A fantastic welcome, mind-blowing, really,' he said.

While always loved off the park, Japan's sharp improvement on the field has them no longer viewed as minnows of the world game. They are a threat to all comers and the sight of the Brave Blossoms fronting up to the haka is something we may just see a lot more of in the years to come.

THE BRAVE BLOSSOMS STARE DOWN THE CHALLENGE / 273

THE MEN WHO SUMMONED THE THUNDER

Opposite Wallaby Nathan Sharpe gets a central view of the haka. TORSTEN BLACKWOOD/AFP VIA GETTY IMAGES

2 August 2008
Eden Park, Auckland

All Blacks 39
(Tony Woodcock 2, Ma'a Nonu 2 tries; Dan Carter 5 pen, 2 con)

Wallabies 10
(Adam Ashley-Cooper try; Matt Giteau pen, con)

All Blacks
15 Mils Muliaina
14 Richard Kahui
13 Conrad Smith
12 Ma'a Nonu
11 Sitiveni Sivivatu
10 Dan Carter
9 Jimmy Cowan
8 Rodney So'oialo
7 Richie McCaw (c)
6 Jerome Kaino
5 Ali Williams
4 Brad Thorn
3 Greg Somerville
2 Andrew Hore
1 Tony Woodcock

Reserves
16 Keven Mealamu
17 John Afoa
18 Anthony Boric
19 Adam Thomson
20 Piri Weepu
21 Stephen Donald
22 Anthony Tuitavake

Wallabies
15 Adam Ashley-Cooper
14 Peter Hynes
13 Stirling Mortlock (c)
12 Berrick Barnes
11 Lote Tuqiri
10 Matt Giteau
9 Luke Burgess
8 Wycliff Palu
7 George Smith
6 Phil Waugh
5 Nathan Sharpe
4 James Horwill
3 Al Baxter
2 Stephen Moore
1 Benn Robinson

Reserves
16 Tatafu Polota-Nau
17 Matt Dunning
18 Dan Vickerman
19 Hugh McMeniman
20 Sam Cordingley
21 Ryan Cross
22 Drew Mitchell

The Wallabies once again find themselves in the one spot they don't want to be: under their own posts. TIM HALES/GETTY IMAGES

'That [touching the ground] was part of that process for me. It was putting a marker in the ground. You are coming to our place. We're going to take you on.'

—NATHAN SHARPE, WALLABIES LOCK

IT'S THE DAY BEFORE the second Bledisloe Cup test in Auckland, 2019, and emotions are running high out on Eden Park. A record number of journalists along the sideline are watching the All Blacks go through their final training run. Almost half of them are Australian, having made the trip across the Tasman because they can taste the blood in the water. They haven't had it on their tongues for a while now, but it's been across the broadsheets and websites in Sydney and Brisbane all week. This could be it, the eve of the day the Wallabies might just get their hands on the Bledisloe Cup after 17 years of waiting.

The Australians managed to pull off one of the great shocks in recent years six days previously, 5300 kilometres to the west. Perth hosted its first Bledisloe Cup test at their new one-billion-dollar stadium, and the Wallabies conspired to put on a performance that made it worth every cent. It was a 47–26 hiding, thanks in no small part to the All Blacks having to play half the game with 14 men after Scott Barrett got sent off. It is the highest score the All Blacks have ever conceded, and in all honesty everyone who was there to see it was in little doubt that it could have been even worse.

It's made for a very tense time. Relations between the All Blacks and the media that year had already been a little fraught, given the expected amount of secrecy and intrigue in the period leading up to the World Cup. The side had two tests before the Perth disaster, a scratchy win over the Pumas in Buenos Aires and then an even scratchier draw against the Springboks back in Wellington, which did little to lower any eyebrows raised at the almighty challenge to be faced later that year: defending their status as world champions.

Now the team is out on the field, doing their usual Friday routine of kicking to each other and casually running through moves. This is the captain's run, where Kieran Read is in charge. They do this the day before every test match, a light run-through to familiarise themselves with the ground and whatever they might be doing differently the next day. There's a big contingent of school children in the South Stand, watching on and eagerly waiting for the All Blacks to finish up and come over for a few autographs and selfies.

A large semi-circle of reporters and camera people has been set up to greet Read as he comes forward to play a straight bat to a series of questions about pressure, not losing on Eden Park for 25 years, and what the Bledisloe Cup means to the All Blacks. It's a big show, especially considering that in Perth only four New Zealand journalists travelled with the team. But while the All Blacks

Opposite The two men who divided New Zealand rugby fans: Graham Henry shakes hands with Robbie Deans.
PHIL WALTER/GETTY IMAGES

captain is wandering across and preparing to face the music, there's a commotion of a different kind going on in another part of town.

A short drive away from the players, their captain, the media and the kids, a room is awash with lubricated conversation. At the Grand Millennium Hotel on Mayoral Drive in the heart of Auckland city, several hundred people are gathered in the main conference room. It's been set up for the Keystone Trust's annual fundraising lunch. The bar was opened at midday, so by the time the special guest speakers get on the microphone, the crowd's ready to be entertained. It's two of the big men of Bledisloe lore: 77-test veteran All Blacks lock Ali Williams and a man he found himself standing alongside at many a lineout over the years, former Wallabies captain Nathan Sharpe, who has 116 tests to his name. Both men's careers go back far enough to when the Wallabies held the Bledisloe Cup.

Sharpe's early career was lived in the not-so-inconsiderable shadow of another Wallabies lock with a haka story to tell. John Eales dominated the Queensland second row throughout the 1990s, so the young Sharpe had to wait for his turn to experience Super 12 rugby. After Eales' retirement in 2001, Sharpe got a crack in the Wallabies and stayed there for an exceptionally long time— commencing in the 2003 Rugby World Cup final, playing 28 consecutive tests across two seasons in 2007–08 and scoring eight test tries.

But when it comes Sharpe's turn to talk, it's a Bledisloe battle from 2008 that he wants to recall. Or, more precisely, the haka that came before it.

Standing at six foot seven and with his bald head free of the scrum cap that he diligently wore for his entire career, Sharpe faces the audience at the Grand Millennium and launches into a story he knows will definitely grab its attention.

IT WAS A RAINY old night in Auckland. The All Blacks were coming off their shock loss in the World Cup the season before, with Graham Henry up in the coaches' box. In the Wallabies' one sat Robbie Deans—and the ongoing story as to why the two men were in their respective seats was dividing the country. NZ Rugby had retained Aucklander Henry despite the All Blacks' worst-ever World Cup performance in 2007, overlooking the credentials of Cantabrian Deans. Once the appointment was made, Deans jumped the ditch and took the Wallabies job. Such was the loyalty to him in the South Island that a shocking number of people in Canterbury pledged their allegiance to Australia rather than the All Blacks as long as the current coaching situation remained.

For the first week of the arrangement, they at least had something to cheer about. The Wallabies came out firing in the first Bledisloe test of 2008, crossing for four tries in a 34–19 rout at ANZ Stadium in Sydney. While the All Blacks were hampered by a couple of key injuries, especially at halfback, they put on an incredibly sloppy display and deserved to be well beaten. This match was a high-water mark of rugby league influence in both sides: a yellow card to Brad Thorn early in the game had freed up space for Ryan Cross to score

the opening try for the Wallabies. Alongside him were Berrick Barnes and Lote Tuqiri, who had both played at the Brisbane Broncos alongside Thorn. Deans had convincingly won the first round of the coaching battle that was dominating talkback radio and the fledgling social media discussions of the time.

One week later, out on the Eden Park field, the Wallabies lined up on their own 10-metre line as the All Blacks prepared for the haka. Sharpe stood shoulder to shoulder with his teammates, as usual the tallest man in the side. He'd been in this position plenty of times before, but had never tasted victory in a test on Eden Park. No Wallaby had since 1986.

His side faced the eastern end of the largest stadium in New Zealand, which would be torn down and rebuilt over the course of the following year and a half in preparation for the next World Cup, as well as an All Blacks team rallying around their kaea, Keven Mealamu.

Ko Aotearoa e ngunguru nei!
It is New Zealand that thunders now!

Just then, as Mealamu called for his side to raise their fists and drop to one knee, Sharpe saw a bolt of lightning crack open the sky behind the All Blacks. A low roll of thunder swept across the ground as the All Blacks completed 'Kapa O Pango'.

'Did you see that?' said Sharpe to no one in particular.

'Yep,' came a reply from one of his teammates.

Sharpe could only be honest in such a moment, when you have perfect clarity about your surroundings. He uttered the two words that summed up his sentiments.

'We're f**ked!'

THE MEN WHO SUMMONED THE THUNDER / 281

Right Singer John Williamson belts out 'Waltzing Matilda' before the start of a Tri Nations match at Stadium Australia in 2001. NICK WILSON/ GETTY IMAGES

THE ROOM AT THE Grand Millennium erupted with laughter. This was the sort of thing they'd paid good money and taken a day off work to hear, and glasses were raised to Sharpe's incisive anecdote. One of those was lifted by the All Black Williams, who was positioned on the edge of the niho that night in 2008 and knew exactly why Sharpe was destined to tell that story for the rest of his speaking engagement career.

It was because 80 minutes after the Wallabies lock had uttered those words, the men who summoned the thunder had enacted their revenge. Tony Woodcock, who established a relish for scoring tries against the Australians, bashed his way over the line after 20 minutes. The prop had run a perfect line on to Jimmy Cowan's pass, but he wasn't content with just the one. He collected the ball off a 22-metre drop-out and smashed his way over again. While the Wallabies managed to pull one back through a nice pass by their veteran captain Stirling Mortlock to a flying Adam Ashley-Cooper, normal service resumed in the second half. This time it was a more traditional ball-runner that put the All Blacks even further ahead. Ma'a Nonu crossed for a double of his own, and when added to Dan Carter's conversions and five penalty goals, it made for a convincing 39–10 scoreline. Every time the All Blacks made a break, the crowd rumbled like the thunder that had amplified the haka.

Sharpe's post-haka prediction was spot-on. Eden Park remained the fortress and whatever confidence that Deans and the Wallabies had gained from the weekend before was dashed as

The use of 'Waltzing Matilda' to counter the haka had been going on for almost a decade when the Wallabies played at home. In fact, it worked like a charm the first time that the Australian Rugby Union employed country singer John Williamson to lead a then world-record crowd at Sydney's Stadium Australia to sing the traditional tune before the Bledisloe Cup match in 1999. The Wallabies handed the All Blacks their heaviest defeat ever, a 28-7 loss, then went on to win the World Cup later that year. However, the iconic song about a hunted criminal in the Australian outback, written in 1895 by poet Banjo Paterson, wasn't universally popular. World Rugby banned the Williamson-led performances for the 2003 World Cup, held in Australia. Before the 2008 test in Brisbane, former Wallabies captain and now commentator Phil Kearns could barely contain his contempt for the rendition, saying sarcastically on air: 'I'm sure that terrifies them [the opposition], a song about a bloke knocking off a sheep and then drowning himself.'

they tramped off the damp field, knowing that they would be facing an even tougher challenge a month later when the two sides met for the Bledisloe decider in Brisbane. The difference this time was that the Wallabies would show up and meet it head on, giving fans on both sides of the Tasman a test match to remember.

THE THIRD BLEDISLOE CUP test of 2008 was played in much more pleasant conditions than the second. The warm, dry night at Suncorp Stadium suited the Wallabies just fine as they ran out to try to win back the oversized trophy that had eluded their grasp for the past five years, led by Mortlock once more. The All Blacks met them on halfway with 'Kapa O Pango' again, with the Australian crowd responding with a rendition of 'Waltzing Matilda'.

The first 10 minutes of the game was a tight affair, and it took a bit of smart thinking by All Blacks halfback Jimmy Cowan to break the deadlock. The Southlander took a quick tap from a scrum free kick on the Wallabies' 22, racing up to the five-metre line and exposing a huge overlap out on the open side. From there, it was just a case of passing the ball through the hands for Mils Muliaina to score. But the Wallabies weren't about to roll over, matching the All Blacks all the way to the half-time break. Matt Giteau launched a cross-kick into the All Blacks' 22 for Peter Hynes to leap up and bat down to a flying Adam Ashley-Cooper, who scored in the corner and gave the Wallabies a 10–7 lead at the break.

The Aussies had one hand on the Bledisloe Cup. That grip got a little tighter when Sharpe's locking partner James Horwill dived over in the corner for a fine try to give them a 10-point lead. Unfortunately for the Aussies, this was going to be one of those moments when Dan Carter decided to show everyone just why he'd be regarded as one of the greatest players ever, and also when Tony Woodcock proved why he'd go down in history as a prop forward with a knack for scoring extremely important test tries.

It was Cowan again who provided the spark, getting the ball in a messy situation on the Wallabies' 10-metre line. He flung a cut-out pass to Conrad Smith, who drew and passed to Woodcock who for some reason was hanging out on the wing. While his tries in the previous test were befitting of a man his size, this time Woodcock found himself with 25 metres to travel and three Wallabies defenders to outpace. Incredibly, that's exactly what the 120-kilogram prop did, gunning it into the corner with an elegant dive that would have made Joe Rokocoko proud.

Shortly afterwards, Piri Weepu came on and scored in the same spot to give the All Blacks their first lead of the match. It came after a masterful display of game management by Carter, who had kicked smartly and organised his backs to get the All Blacks into a position to strike. As the clock ticked towards full-time, Carter then did it himself, scoring under the posts to make the score 28–17. Sharpe and his Wallabies weren't finished, however. Three minutes from time, the ex-league man Cross came flying on to a short ball 10 metres out from the All Blacks' line and scored to close the gap to four points. But, try as they might, the hosts couldn't crack the All Blacks' defence to snatch the lead before the hooter went.

The 28–24 win after the two sides had taken turns crushing one another in the two preceding tests was the closest the All Blacks have come to losing the Bledisloe Cup during their seemingly unending reign since 2003. As of 2020, only one Bledisloe series since has gone to a deciding test. The All Blacks and the Wallabies did face each other one more time in 2008 in Hong Kong, but it was designated as part of both

Opposite top Ali Williams reminds Nathan Sharpe that he's right there. MATT KING/ GETTY IMAGES

Opposite below Ma'a Nonu crunches into a big Wallaby tackle. HANNAH PETERS/ GETTY IMAGES

sides' end-of-year tour schedules (the All Blacks won 19–14).

However, Sharpe wasn't done when it came to the haka, although it would take until his final Bledisloe battle to come up with something a bit more effective than cursing at the juxtaposition of nature and man's fury. In 2012, the Wallabies found themselves ready to face the All Blacks at Suncorp Stadium again. The first test in Sydney had been won 27–19 by the All Blacks, the second 22–0 at Eden Park. Sharpe had been unceremoniously dropped the year before by Deans and missed the 2011 World Cup semi-final, which would have been his 100th test. But the subsequent World Cup failure spooked Deans into rightfully thinking that his job was on the line the next season, so Sharpe suddenly found himself back in the frame. Not only was he in the starting line-up, but also he was made captain.

The situation for the Wallabies was dire. No one gave them any chance of beating an All Blacks side that had won every game so far under new coach Steve Hansen and had also stretched their winning streak that started the year before to 14 tests. Sharpe now had to lead his men out to face that force, but he had a plan to counter the haka with a show of unity in the changing room.

Sharpe told his team to circle up, take a knee and touch the ground.

'I figured the All Blacks would do the "Kapa O Pango", where they put their hand on the ground,' he explained. 'I thought it was symbolic for us to say, well, they're coming into our country so we are going to put hands down on our ground first. At the start of the week for us, we spoke about drawing a line in the sand. That [touching the ground] was part of that process for me. It was putting a marker in the ground. You are coming to our place. We're going to take you on.'

That's exactly what the Wallabies did that night in Brisbane. It wasn't like the pulsating 2008 encounter, with no tries scored by either side. The hosts led 12–6 at half-time but the score remained locked at 18-all at the end, with the All Blacks once again relying on Carter, who this time scored all their points with six penalties.

Nathan Sharpe retired from test rugby at the end of that year, with 116 caps to his name. Seven years later and a day after he made the crowd at the Grand Millennium roar with laughter at his blunt response to the thunder-summoning haka, his old side went out to try to win the Bledisloe Cup on Eden Park. They had confidence after their big win in Perth the week before. They had the players to do the job and a fired-up coach seething with ambition in Michael Cheika. They stood and faced the haka just as Sharpe himself had done so many times in his career.

The All Blacks didn't care, and flogged them 36–0.

ACKNOWLEDGEMENTS

Andy

I would like to acknowledge the team from New Zealand Rugby for their support and belief in this project. Thanks to David Barton-Ginger and Ged Mahony for being inspirational leaders and always looking for opportunities for their people to grow. Big ups to the digital content crew for picking up the slack when I have been tucked away in meeting rooms working on another chapter. Massive respect to Harriet Anderson from VBM for her support, knowledge and always positive attitude. As a Pākehā writing a book about the haka, this simply wouldn't have been possible without the guidance, wisdom and constant encouragement of Luke Crawford. Kia ora!

Shout out to Michael 'Pencil' Watson, one of the most passionate rugby fans I know, for the initial chats which helped spark the idea for this book.

To my co-writer Jamie, it has been an inspirational process working with you and I hope we can collaborate again in the future.

And finally, thanks to my family—baby Briana and Carla—love always.

Jamie

Massive thanks to all the photographers who, for well over a century, have provided us with amazing images of the All Blacks and the haka.

Once again, a huge thank you to Stephen Berg and the team at the New Zealand Rugby Museum in Palmerston North. Much love and respect to Allen & Unwin who have done an awesome job getting this project over the line, Mike Wagg for his editing, and the Remuera Public Library for providing me with a place to work.

Special mention to Emily Scarratt, Ruby Tui, Sarah Hirini, Clark Laidlaw and Kurt Baker for their time, and a lot of gratitude to New Zealand Rugby for letting me into the fold and achieving this goal—especially Andy for his hard work and trust.

Opposite Players shake hands after the autumn international between New Zealand and England at Twickenham in November 2018. The All Blacks emerged with a 1-point victory. BEN STANSALL/AFP VIA GETTY IMAGES

Following page The haka sets the scene for an encounter between the All Blacks and England at Twickenham in November 2018. STEVE BARDENS/THE RFU COLLECTION VIA GETTY IMAGES

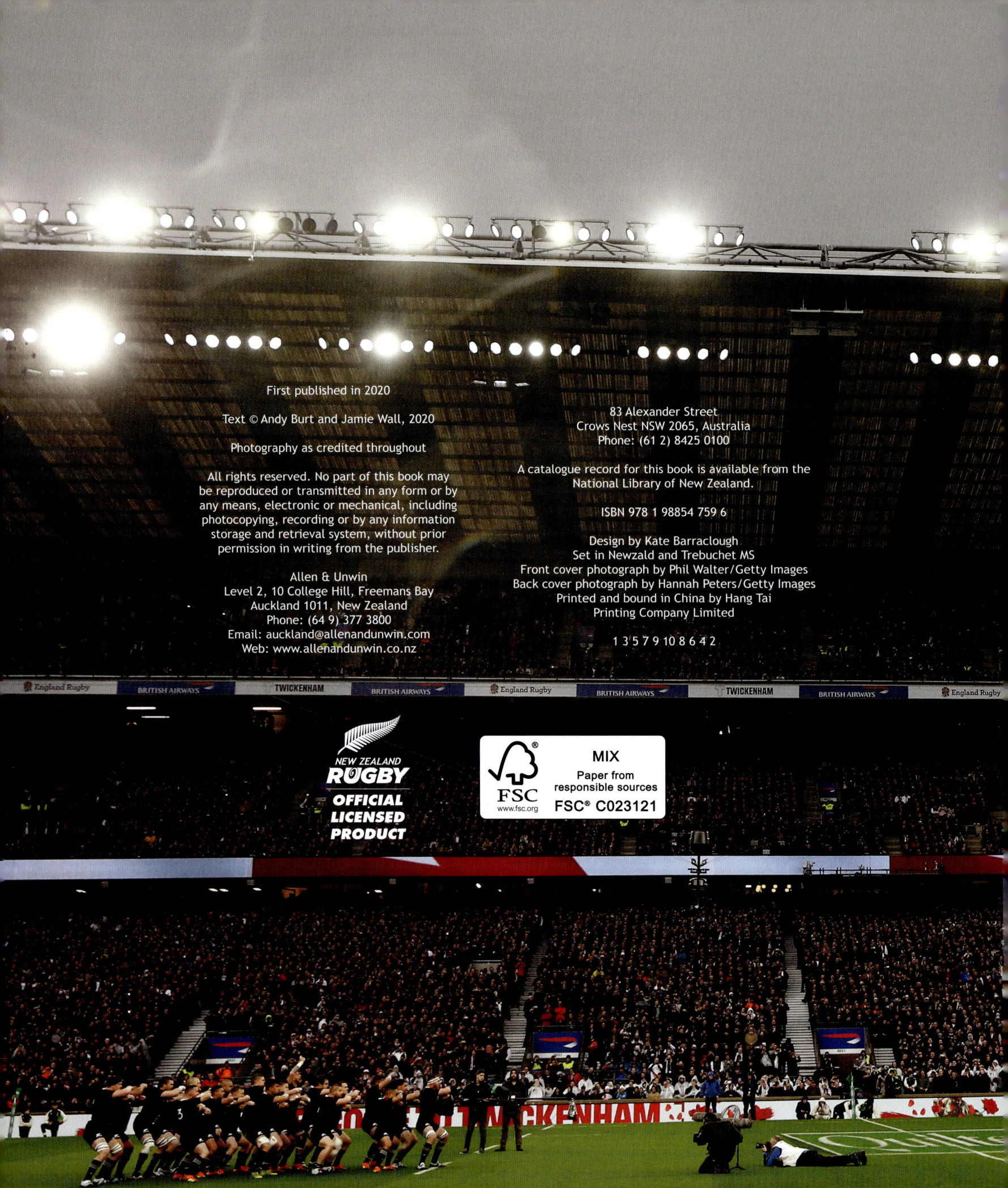

First published in 2020

Text © Andy Burt and Jamie Wall, 2020

Photography as credited throughout

All rights reserved. No part of this book may be reproduced or transmitted in any form or by any means, electronic or mechanical, including photocopying, recording or by any information storage and retrieval system, without prior permission in writing from the publisher.

Allen & Unwin
Level 2, 10 College Hill, Freemans Bay
Auckland 1011, New Zealand
Phone: (64 9) 377 3800
Email: auckland@allenandunwin.com
Web: www.allenandunwin.co.nz

83 Alexander Street
Crows Nest NSW 2065, Australia
Phone: (61 2) 8425 0100

A catalogue record for this book is available from the National Library of New Zealand.

ISBN 978 1 98854 759 6

Design by Kate Barraclough
Set in Newzald and Trebuchet MS
Front cover photograph by Phil Walter/Getty Images
Back cover photograph by Hannah Peters/Getty Images
Printed and bound in China by Hang Tai Printing Company Limited

1 3 5 7 9 10 8 6 4 2